EVANGELISM BY THE BOOK

Evangelism by the Book

13 Biblical Methods

Tom Stebbins

CHRISTIAN PUBLICATIONS
CAMP HILL, PENNSYLVANIA

Christian Publications
3825 Hartzdale Drive, Camp Hill, PA 17011

The mark of ✝ *vibrant faith*

ISBN: 0-87509-473-2
LOC Catalog Card Number: 91-58237
© 1991 by Christian Publications
All rights reserved
Printed in the United States of America

91 92 93 94 95 5 4 3 2 1

Cover Design: Step One Design

CONTENTS

Foreword

I N SPITE OF ALL THE BOOKS on evangelism,
there is always room for one more. *Provided*
it is predicated on personal conviction tested
and proved on the spiritual battlefield where
only those venture forth who earnestly contend
for the faith.

Evangelism by the Book easily qualifies. Tom
Stebbins, a faithful minister of the gospel,
learned the hard way—in the villages of war-
torn Vietnam—that God wants to transform
His servants not simply into personal evangelists but into *trainers* of personal evangelists.
For many years Tom has demonstrated his zeal
and competency in evangelism as a pastor of
evangelism in Hong Kong and Omaha, Nebraska, as well as a clinic teacher for Evangelism
Explosion International and a member of its international board.

In this highly readable book, the author explains how he discovered God's multiplication
factor in fruit-bearing. He does so in a marvelous application of biblical principles and illustrations. He marshals anecdote, personal
testimony and Scripture to weave a fascinating

1

progression of argument into a clear and believable conclusion. At no time is the treatment heavy-handed. Tom's brilliant sense of organization and genuine feel for rich good humor see to that.

Unflaggingly practical, *Evangelism by the Book* focuses on you—your personal needs and aspirations. Step by step Tom will convince you that if you dare to dream the dream of Christ-centered living, you will see God do through you unbelievable evangelistic and discipling exploits.

Training witnesses to train witnesses. I have found that to be the key to successful evangelism. So has Tom Stebbins, and he tells you about it in a way that can change your life.

D. James Kennedy
Founder and President
Evangelism Explosion III International

Introduction

ACTUALLY, I HAD NO INTENTION of authoring a book about evangelism. But I was in Mechanicsburg, Pennsylvania, delivering a series of messages on the biblical basis for evangelism, and Dr. K. Neill Foster, the executive vice president of Christian Publications, heard me speak.

"Tom," he said to me over lunch, "I think you have a book that needs to be written."

My mind flashed back briefly to my years as a missionary in Vietnam and those frantic days in March, 1975, as we evacuated people by helicopter from the roof of the American embassy while the country collapsed around us. "Yes, Neill, I've been wanting to write a book about my narrow escape from Vietnam."

"No, Tom," Neill said decisively. "We'll get to that later. Let's do the one on evangelism first."

So here it is. It is the essence of what I have learned in 40 years of "grass roots" evangelism, the discipling of new believers and the on-the-job training of evangelists. It is laced with Scripture—our one authoritative guide to

God's will for us—and with personal anecdotes to inspire and challenge.

I've purposely made the book 13 chapters long so that you can use it also as the text for a Sunday school quarter or a week-night course on personal evangelism.

In addition to thanking Dr. Foster for launching me on this venture, I pay tribute to Mrs. Ruth Cozette for her assistance in typing, to H. Robert Cowles for his thoughtful and thorough editing, and to my wife, Donna, who has patiently endured my preoccupation these past months.

Dwight L. Moody, the great 19th-century evangelist, told of seeing a painting he liked very much. It was of a drowning man clinging with both hands to the cross. Later he saw a painting he liked even more. It, too, was of a drowning man. One arm was around the cross, the other was reaching out to a fellow victim in the water.

The most significant day of my life occurred in the summer of 1942 when, clinging to the cross of Christ, *I was rescued by Jesus* from a sea of sin and eternal death. The second most significant day occurred eight years later when I realized why God had saved me. I had been saved not just to escape hell and enjoy heaven but *so I could rescue others*. For more than 40 years it has been my privilege to be directly involved in such a rescue mission.

But midway in that mission a third "great

beginning" took place. It has impacted my life and work as much as the previous two. It has brought me to a ministry literally "beyond my wildest dreams." I saw that God intended me not only to win people, but to *train people to win others*.

This book is about those three beginnings. But it is not simply testimony. I intend it to be a challenge as well. You, the reader, whatever your station or age, can have a similarly fulfilling life and ministry.

Really.

Louise, in Fort Worth, Texas, might have supposed she could not. But she signed up anyway at Gambrell Street Baptist Church for training in personal evangelism. She completed level one and advanced to become a trainer of others.

The following semester two seminary students who were assigned to her team retreated to the presiding pastor. "Brother Dan, you need to put us with someone else. We are here to learn to be evangelists, and this woman surely can't teach us."

Pastor Dan assured the students that Louise could indeed train them. He encouraged them to stay with her for two weeks. If after that they wanted a different trainer, he would comply.

By the end of the semester, the team had led eight persons to faith in Christ. Neither of the seminary students would give up Louise. Jesus Christ was clearly evident in her life. When she went to visit, no one ever turned her away from their door. Louise was a gifted personal evangelist and a committed trainer.

Louise is also in her mid-70s—and clinically blind!

Enough said. Proceed to Chapter 1.

Thomas H. Stebbins
Omaha, Nebraska

CHAPTER 1

Liberating Captive People

Psalm 126

TAKING OFF FROM THE SAIGON airport, our pilot nosed the single-engine Fairchild Porter northwest across South Vietnam's delta. He gained altitude as quickly as possible to avoid sniper fire from below, for Vietnam was at war.

Tom, I said to myself, *this could be your last day on planet earth*! But my apprehension about flying over enemy-held territory was checked as I remembered again my mission. I was en route to take the good news of Jesus Christ to tribal villages that had never heard it.

Gradually the multi-checkered rice paddies below us blended into dark green rows of rubber trees. These, in turn, became majestic, jungle-covered foothills marred only by the craters and landslides left from American B-52 bombing raids.

My preoccupation with the panorama below us was abruptly halted as our pilot cut the engine and began his descent to the little provincial capital of An-Loc. Shortly we were bumping across the landing strip. Pastor Dieu-Huynh, driving a borrowed Jeep, was there to meet me.

Dieu-Huynh was one of a handful of Stieng Montagnards who had believed in Christ Jesus while studying to become government cadres. Concerned about the destiny of his 100,000 fellow tribespeople, Dieu-Huynh deliberately gave up his plans for civil service and instead enrolled at Nhatrang Bible Institute to become a pastor-evangelist.

Upon his graduation in 1970, he visited me at our Saigon mission headquarters. He invited me to help him evangelize the first Stieng villages.

"But Dieu-Huynh," I countered, "I don't speak your tribal language. What help can I be?"

The young preacher waved off my hesitancy. "That's no problem," he assured me. "You preach in Vietnamese, and I'll interpret into Stieng."

Too good to refuse

It was an invitation I could not refuse! From age 17 when God called me to serve Him, I had wanted to be a pioneer missionary like William Carey, David Livingstone or Hudson Taylor. I had dreamed about invading the frontiers of populous India, mid-Africa or inland China. Suddenly, a century after those heroes had passed from the scene, Dieu-Huynh was offering me the opportunity I had until then only dreamed of.

I climbed into the Jeep with Dieu-Huynh, who coaxed the aging vehicle over the nondescript provincial roads toward the four Stieng villages we were scheduled to visit. As the vehicle groaned over the crest of a particularly steep hill, I spied in the distance the first village. Smoke was rising from each of the long-houses built on stilts to protect from mosquitoes and tigers.

The sound of our approaching Jeep attracted a crowd of bare-breasted women and naked children, soon joined by G-stringed men. Some snickered at their first sight of a white man. Others looked on in wide-eyed wonder. By the time we had set up our battery-operated public address system, some 200 villagers had gathered under the shade trees in the center of the village.

Dieu-Huynh greeted the people in their own language. I could not understand what he was saying, but clearly he had the attention of the villagers. I assumed he was introducing me, for he ended his comments by handing the microphone to me.

Suddenly, it was my turn! At last, my dream of pioneering an evangelistic thrust into one of the world's remaining unreached tribes had come true. I could hardly believe it! The message I had carefully prepared seemed suddenly inadequate. How should I begin? What could I say to people who had never even once heard the beautiful name of Jesus Christ, my Savior?

I kept the message simple enough for a five-year-old to grasp. Sentence by sentence, Dieu-Huynh interpreted for me. The people seemed to understand. I could tell by the look on their faces. But had I said enough? What kind of a response should I expect? Should I invite them to trust in my Savior?

Everyone stood up

Unsure what to do, I said falteringly, "If you'd like to receive God's Son as your Savior, please stand." To my surprise, all my listeners, to a person, rose to their feet!

"Dieu-Huynh," I said, "I'm afraid they don't understand. Have them sit down again while we clarify for them what is involved in such a commitment."

I repeated the gospel message, emphasizing repentance, and Dieu-Huynh interpreted my remarks. We told the villagers their fetishes and blood sacrifices would have to go.

Then, for the second time, I extended an invitation to those who wanted to receive God's Son as their Savior. Again, everyone stood.

Puzzled, I asked Dieu-Huynh to explain the gospel further to them and to pray with them in small groups.

In the next village, I gave the same message. No one responded. The people were not ready to give up their ancient animistic ways. In the third village, when I mentioned burning fetishes and giving up their rice whiskey, half the people rose to return to their long-houses. It was evident they also were not yet ready to follow Christ.

The sun at high noon was very warm when we reached the fourth village. So the villagers invited us into their makeshift palaver house. They sat shoulder-to-shoulder on the mud floor, knees tight under their chins, the backs of one row up against the knees of the next.

The bearded, balding village chief sat in the very center of the crowd. In the intense heat, I could see the perspiration pouring from his body. But neither the heat nor the press of people seemed to matter. Everyone was intent on what I had to say. It was the first time they had heard such good news. Their excitement was undeniable.

As I extended an invitation to these Montagnards to put their faith in Jesus Christ, the unexpected happened. The chief, who served as spokesman for the village, stood up. He shook his fists in the air, at the same time shouting something at the top of his lungs. The villagers responded in like fashion.

"What are they shouting?" I asked Dieu-Huynh.

He explained. "You asked, 'Who wants to trust Jesus Christ as Savior?' and they are shouting, '*We* do! *We* do!'"

Never before or since have I witnessed such an enthusiastic response to the gospel. And to think this was happening in the mountain jungles of Vietnam in a village that had never before heard of Jesus! Chills coursed from the top of my head to the very ends of my toes. It had to be the most thrilling day of my life!

Sometime in eternity, I believe I will look back through the corridors of time to that day and say to God, "Thank you for such a privilege! That one day of pioneer evangelism was worth all the difficulties of my life on earth. Thank you for giving me a ministry fulfilling beyond my wildest dreams!"

Each of us enjoys an exciting dream. Even more, we like to see those dreams become reality.

The basic premise of this book is this: *God desires that every believer obey His Son's Great Commission to make disciples; if we follow the biblical guidelines for disciple-making, we can discover a ministry unimaginably fulfilling—beyond our wildest dreams.*

Biblical guidelines:

In this chapter and those that follow, I shall set down those biblical guidelines.

We begin with Psalm 126:

> When the LORD brought back the captives
>   to Zion,
>   we were like men who dreamed.
> Our mouths were filled with laughter,
>   our tongues with songs of joy.
> Then it was said among the nations,
>   "The LORD has done great things for
>   them."
> The LORD has done great things for us,
>   and we are filled with joy.
>
> Restore our fortunes, O LORD,
>   like streams in the Negev.
> Those who sow in tears
>   will reap with songs of joy.
> He who goes out weeping,
>   carrying seed to sow,
> will return with songs of joy,
>   carrying sheaves with him.

In 1956, when my wife Donna and I prepared to go as missionaries to Vietnam, we selected the last two verses of that Psalm, beginning with "Those who sow in tears," as a foundation for our service. As we look back through the years, we realize we could not have chosen a more appropriate Scripture.

Psalm 126 alludes to the great things God did to liberate His captive people. They were things so amazing that the Israelites thought they were dreaming. The Psalm can be divided into four parts, each setting forth a very significant facet of the evangelistic task committed to us: a return, a rejoicing, a request and a reaping.

1. A Return

First, there is the return. Psalm 126 is one of 15 "Songs of Ascents" which great companies of Hebrew travelers sang as they ascended to Mount Zion for the annual festivals. The Psalm describes the joy of the Israelites as they returned from Babylonian captivity to their beloved homeland.

> When the Lord brought back the captives
>   to Zion,
>   we were like men who dreamed.
>   (verse 1)

Evangelism in this context might be defined as the exciting task of bringing the message of emancipation to enslaved people. Evangelism is the glorious business of delivering sinners from Satan, sin and eternal death. For me among the Montagnards of South Vietnam, it was the thrilling enterprise of liberating aborigines from the enslaving power of rice whiskey, superstitious blood sacrifices and the paralyzing fear of evil spirits.

But a person does not have to live in pagan

lands to appreciate the liberating power of the gospel. I was privileged to be born into a godly Christian family. And although from birth I attended church regularly, I too needed to be liberated. I was one of those described in Hebrews 2:15 "who all their lives were held in slavery by their fear of death."

From as far back as I can remember, I went to bed fearing death. I dreamed at night of death. Even in the daylight hours when I encountered the slightest danger, I trembled at the thought of death. Once on a ship at sea, the fire alarm sounded. I did not know it was simply a practice drill. As passengers donned life jackets and ran for the lifeboats, I thought the ship was actually sinking. My heart almost stopped at the awful prospect of death at sea.

Freed at last

Fear of death continued to plague my life until one day at a youth conference in Nyack, New York, Evangelist Merv Roselle announced the most marvelous, liberating news I had ever heard. He told how through faith in the Lord Jesus Christ and by trusting in His atoning death and glorious resurrection, I could receive the gift of eternal life.

That night, at my mother's side, I received Christ Jesus into my life as my Savior. And Jesus, through His indwelling presence and the assurance of His Word, freed me from the fear of death that had enslaved me. Through the en-

suing years, especially during 18 years in war-
torn Vietnam, I encountered many close calls
with death. But the fear of death is gone! I am
ready to die. Now I have a bold confidence that
if I die, I will move from an abundant, purposeful life here on earth to an even more
glorious life with God in heaven.

Have *you* "returned" from your captivity to
sin, Satan and death? Have *you* found the
abundant, purposeful eternal life Jesus Christ
offers? Do *you* know for certain that if your life
were to end today, you would go immediately
to be with Christ Jesus in heaven? Have *you*
ever personally received Him as your Savior
and Lord?

If your answer is "No" or "I don't know," I
ask you to pause right now and think seriously
about the matter. Turn now, before reading any
farther, to page 330 and the section entitled
"Do You Know for Sure?" The instructions
there will help you take the most important
step of your life. The rest of this chapter and
the chapters that follow will not make much
sense until you do.

2. A Rejoicing

We move on to the second facet of the evangelistic task set forth by the psalmist. Evangelism—biblical evangelism—brings abundant
joy. The writer describes that joy quite aptly
when he says,

Our mouths were filled with laughter,
our tongues with songs of joy.
Then it was said among the nations,
"The LORD has done great things for
them."
The LORD has done great things for us,
and we are filled with joy. (126:2–3)

Nothing surpasses the ecstasy of one coming out of prison doors to breathe again the fresh air of freedom. No sensation compares with the delight a captive experiences to return from a foreign land to his family and home. He pinches himself and asks, "Can this be true? Or am I just dreaming?"

No greater rejoicing

Likewise in the spiritual realm, there is no greater cause for rejoicing than the emancipation of a man or woman from slavery to Satan, sin and death. God rejoices, the angels in heaven rejoice, the redeemed sinner rejoices and the evangelist rejoices.

Over dinner one evening in the home of mutual friends, Peggy recalled some of the joy she experienced in leading her friend Dorothy to Christ. The two had attended Bible Study Fellowship together for two and a half years. One day Peggy invited Dorothy home for lunch. As the two conversed, Dorothy asked, "What does it mean to do God's will?" Peggy tried to explain. "You have to surrender your

life to God and trust in Christ as your Savior."
Then the two knelt in Peggy's living room by
the coffee table and Dorothy invited Christ into
her heart as Savior and surrendered her life to
Him as Lord.

Fruit in her basket

The next day at the Bible Study Fellowship,
the leader saw Peggy's face aglow and asked,
"Who's in your fruit basket?" Without Peggy
saying a word, the leader could detect her unusual joy and correctly guessed that it came
from her leading someone to Christ.

The evangelist's rejoicing eclipses that of all
other achievements because of its eternal and
divine dimensions. The Olympic athlete
rejoices in a gold medal that he or she, after a
brief time of ecstasy, tucks away in a trophy
case and seldom thinks of.

Those who gain their satisfaction from riches,
fame, political power and the best of earth's
pleasures discover that these things are temporal. But the evangelist's exhilaration only in-
creases with time and in eternity.

Athletes admittedly find a measure of
gratification in the thought that their feats were
achieved through personal ability and strength.
But how much more exciting to know that God
by His Spirit working through our humble, im-
perfect witness has saved a person forever!
How much more fulfilling to acknowledge
with the psalmist:

> The Lord has done great things for us,
> and we are filled with joy. (126:3)

Mark, a member of Christ Community Church in Omaha, where I am associate pastor for outreach, will tell you that once you have experienced the joy of leading a person to Christ, you will never be the same. As a new Christian, Mark had begun attending the church.

One Sunday morning he heard about the start of a new 16-week semester of Evangelism Explosion training. (Evangelism Explosion is a systematic method, pioneered by Dr. D. James Kennedy of Fort Lauderdale, Florida, for leading another person into saving faith in Jesus Christ. As you will discover, I am an enthusiastic proponent of Evangelism Explosion because it works so well.) On his way out of church that morning Mark had a question for our senior pastor, Rev. Robert L. Thune.

Could I qualify?

"Pastor, could a young Christian like me qualify for that evangelism training?" Mark asked.

With Pastor Bob's encouragement, Mark enlisted, purchased the notebook of materials, and prepared for the first class session by memorizing a very brief gospel outline. After the first lesson he thought to himself, *I've got to try this!* The next day at work, during coffee and lunch breaks and whenever he could squeeze in a few words, he shared the gospel with a fellow employee. On Saturday evening while I was at the church preparing for our monthly family film night, I heard someone approaching noisily down the hall. It was Mark.

"Pastor!" he exclaimed exuberantly. "I'll never be the same! With God's help I did it! I led my first person to Christ! I'm going to do this the rest of my life! There's just nothing like it, Pastor!"

Peggy and Mark are only two among hundreds who in leading people out of sin's captivity to freedom in Christ Jesus have found a fulfilling ministry surpassing their wildest dreams. Others like them have met me in the parking lot of the church with similar glowing reports. Some have come into my office bursting with joy. Still others have called me at home because they just could not wait to share their most recent exciting adventure in personal evangelism.

I have observed something encouraging in all this rejoicing. To discover a fulfilling, life-transforming ministry, it is not absolutely necessary to cross an ocean, learn a foreign language, penetrate deep into jungle villages. Wherever God puts you, in whatever situation you find yourself—but especially among family, friends, neighbors, work associates and casual acquaintances—you can find satisfying opportunities for personal evangelism.

3. A Request

That brings us to the third facet of the evangelistic task set forth by the psalmist. He voices a request:

> Restore our fortunes, O LORD,
>   like streams in the Negev. (126:4)

As those former Israelite captives rejoiced in God's deliverance, their minds went back to fellow-countrymen still in Babylon. With their joy tempered by sorrow, they prayed in effect, "Lord, please save the rest of our captive people."

The imagery employed in their request is full of meaning. "Like streams in the Negev" was a reference to the arid south, dependent upon melting mountain snow for water. In the winter months, the streams had but a trickle of water for the Negev, but as warm summer sun melted the mountain snow, the streams gushed with life-giving water. Hence the Israelites prayed that God would cause the trickle of captives whom He had brought from Babylon to swell into a great flood of liberated people.

In verse 5 the psalmist employs more imagery as he alludes to this deliverance:

> Those who sow in tears
>   will reap with songs of joy.

In response to Israel's compassionate intercession, the psalmist envisions captives, like a
handful of seed, becoming a great harvest of
sheaves. And this in answer to prayer.

Prayer is the key

Throughout the Scriptures we find this same
emphasis on prayer. In Psalm 2:8, we overhear
God the Father calling His Son to prayer:

> Ask of me,
>> and I will make the nations your
>>> inheritance,
>> the ends of the earth your possession.

And Jesus, throughout His earthly ministry,
did just that. He spent hours in quiet or remote
places praying to the Father for the advance of
His kingdom.

In the book of Acts there are more references
to praying than to preaching. The reason? The
early church advanced on its knees.

Paul's "heart's desire and prayer" for the Israelites was that "they may be saved" (Romans
10:1). So intense was his prayer for his un-
redeemed kinsmen that he said, "I have great
sorrow and unceasing anguish in my heart. For
I could wish that I myself were cursed and cut
off from Christ for the sake of my brothers,
those of my own race, the people of Israel"
(Romans 9:2–4).

Seeing the power of prayer in his own ministry, Paul wrote to his disciple, Timothy, "I urge, then, first of all, that requests, prayers, intercession and thanksgiving be made for everyone. . . . This is good, and pleases God our Savior, who wants all men to be saved and to come to a knowledge of the truth" (1 Timothy 2:1–4).

Prayer has been the secret of modern-day missionary advance. See David Brainerd in the woods of colonial America pouring out his very soul before God for the perishing Indians, without whose salvation he could not be content. Listen to Edward Payson as he exhorts: "Prayer is the first thing, the second thing, the third thing necessary. . . . Pray, then, my dear brother. Pray, pray, pray." Read what E.M. Bounds writes: "What the church needs today is not more machinery or better, not new organizations or more novel methods, but men whom the Holy Spirit can use—men of prayer."

We evangelize only as well as we pray

Payson and Bounds are right. Throughout church history prayer has always greatly impacted evangelism. Indeed, so much so that it can be said we have evangelized only as well as we have prayed.

The evangelist who prays will become, by God's design, the one who reaps eternal results. The interceding church will become the harvesting church. It is no accident that the church in Korea, known for its unusual prayer life, has become today one of the fastest growing churches in the world.

My 24 years of missionary work in Vietnam, Guam and Hong Kong taught me that little prayer results in little blessing; much prayer, much blessing; great volumes of prayer, revival and people movements toward Christ Jesus.

In 1988 I took a team of five to Capital City Alliance Church in Manila to teach and train at an Evangelism Explosion clinic. While there I met a dear Filipino woman, Mrs. Lourdes. For nine years she had been praying for a friend, her friend's doctor-husband and another friend's engineer-husband. Every Sunday she would put a prayer request for these three unsaved people in the offering plate. And each week the pastoral staff of the church would pray for Mrs. Lourdes' three unsaved friends.

During our week in her church, a member of our evangelism team made a point to share the gospel with these three people Mrs. Lourdes had been praying for. *All three* invited Christ into their lives as Savior and Lord! God had answered prayer.

Kim, a young woman in our Omaha church, prayed for seven years for the salvation of her best friend's husband. One night while training high school youth in evangelism, Kim felt led to take her team of three to visit her friend and her friend's husband, both of whom were by then 29 years old. According to the training schedule, it was her 14-year-old team member's turn to present the gospel. Kim prayed as her trainee began to share. She marveled at the husband's interest. As the evening came to a close, this man invited Christ into his life. Again, the power of prayer was illustrated.

Do you long to discover a ministry more fulfilling than you could dream? If so, such a ministry must incorporate effectual, fervent prayer. Like liberated Israel, you must lay before your great God your urgent requests.

4. A Reaping

We come to the last facet of the evangelistic task set forth by the writer of Psalm 126: the time of reaping.

> Those who sow in tears
>   will reap with songs of joy.
> He who goes out weeping,
>   carrying seed to sow,
> will return with songs of joy,
>   carrying sheaves with him. (5–6)

With those two verses as the biblical foundation for our missionary and pastoral service, Donna and I discovered God leading us to focus our efforts more and more on evangelism. As we did so, we noticed an amazing thing. Whether we preached to crowds or witnessed one-on-one, whether overseas or here in

North America, we saw God's law of the harvest at work: "Whoever sows sparingly will also reap sparingly, and whoever sows generously will also reap generously" (2 Corinthians 9:6).

When, like seed, God's Word is sown in human hearts, it has the potential to produce life and fruitfulness. But, as in agriculture, the sower must expend a large amount of labor and patience before he or she can reap a harvest.

Mark, the young man in Omaha whom I referred to earlier, heard that the woman across the street from where he lived was dying of cancer. One day he went over to visit her and to offer her the gift of eternal life. Although she listened attentively, she refused Mark's invitation to trust Christ. Mark was disappointed. Several months later in the hospital, however, the seed of God's Word began to grow. The woman called a Christian friend to come and tell her how she could prepare for heaven. Just before she died, she received Christ as her Savior. She asked her friend to contact Mark and thank him for earlier sharing the gospel with her.

Middle-of-the-night rejoicing

While we were in Guam in 1975–76, Donna and I befriended a couple about our age who were caught up in a false cult. The husband built boats. And since we needed some fishing boats for Vietnamese refugees, we spent much time together. On a number of occasions, Donna and I witnessed to the couple, but the Word of God did not appear to have any impact on their lives.

One night, some 10 years later, we were awakened in Omaha by a telephone call from this couple in Guam. Although it was two o'clock in the morning, Omaha time, they could not wait to give us the good news. They had just invited Jesus Christ into their lives! How we rejoiced—even at two in the morning! Our witness many years earlier had at last born fruit. Those who sow the seed of the gospel will somehow, someday, joyfully reap the harvest.

No joy can compare with that of the evangelist's. Nothing brings fulfillment quite like rescuing captives and seeing them delight in the glorious liberty of the children of God!

Most of us have potential for evangelistic ministry far beyond what we think possible. We have not developed that potential simply because our circumstances never demanded it. We limit ourselves not by time, money or other resources, but by not dreaming big enough. God wants to become in us and through us much more than until now we have allowed Him to be.

So what do we do?

First, I suggest you get down on your knees with your Bible open to Jesus' Great Commission (Matthew 28:19–20) and dream big. Dream a dream so large you cannot possibly fulfill it by yourself.

Second, pray. Believe God to do through you as great a thing as He did when He brought the captive Israelites back to their land.

Third, share the gospel personally, faithfully and generously with others. Submit yourself to rigid training that will equip you to evangelize effectively. Then pass that training on to other believers and join hands with them for a great harvest to the glory of God.

Fourth, expect such a harvest. Expect God to do great things in your generation and in your place of life and service—things that will go far beyond your wildest dreams!

In the next chapter, you and I will look at a biblical strategy for developing this kind of fulfilling ministry.

Study Questions

Psalm 126

1. What, more than anything else, do you dream about accomplishing in your lifetime? What practical steps are you taking to see that become a reality?

2. Describe and explain the mixed emotions that the Israelite captives were experiencing (2, 5).

3. What great things had God done for Israel

(2–3) to which even the heathen nations around couldn't close their eyes?

4. How might the return of captives resemble "streams of the Negev" (4) or seed becoming sheaves (6)?

5. What has God done for you that is so great you had to pinch yourself to see if you were dreaming?

6. How does God usually answer prayer in your life: with prompt, speedy replies or through a long planting, cultivating, watering process?

7. Share with one person or pen on one sheet of paper how God set you free from sin's captivity and brought you into glorious freedom and eternal, abundant life through His Son.

8. If you are not able to recall such an experience, turn to the back of this book (p. 330) and study prayerfully "Do You Know For Sure?". Then ask someone whom you know is a believer to help you pray to trust Christ as your Savior.

CHAPTER 2

Mending Torn Nets

Mark 1

TWO FISHERMEN WERE SWAPPING tales and, as often happens, each was trying to top the other's catch.

"I once caught a 300-pound salmon!" boasted the first man.

"Ain't no such fish!" protested the other.

"Well," contended the first, "I caught one. I'll bet you never pulled in a fish that big."

"No," the other man agreed rather meekly. "I haven't had much luck in my fishing. But once I pulled in an old brass lantern. On the bottom it read, 'Property of Christopher Columbus, 1492.' And, amazingly, the lantern was still lit!"

"Hey, wait a minute," countered the first storyteller. "Let's make a deal. I'll knock 200 pounds off my salmon if you'll put out that dumb flame in your lantern!"

Mark in his Gospel tells of four fishermen whom Jesus encountered on the shores of the Sea of Galilee:

> After John was put in prison, Jesus went into Galilee, proclaiming the good news of God. "The time has come, " he said. "The kingdom of God is near. Repent and believe the good news!"
>
> As Jesus walked beside the Sea of Galilee, he saw Simon and his brother Andrew casting a net into the lake, for they were fishermen. "Come, follow me," Jesus said, "and I will make you fishers of men." At once they left their nets and followed him.
>
> When he had gone a little farther, he saw James son of Zebedee and his brother John in a boat, preparing their nets. Without delay he called them, and they left their father Zebedee in the boat with the hired men and followed him. (1:14–20)

I suspect that those four first-century fishermen—Peter, Andrew, James and John—if they were alive today, would have some humorous and even hair-raising stories to tell us. True ones, at that! I do not know what they were talking about when Jesus met them along the shores of the Sea of Galilee. But whatever the subject, Jesus turned their attention to a higher, more fulfilling investment of their lives.

"Come, follow me," Jesus invited, "and I will make you fishers of men."

Many comparisons

The Scriptures employ a variety of metaphors to describe the glorious task of evangelism. We noted two in Psalm 126: rescuing captives and harvesting sheaves. Other Bible comparisons include winning a race, finding lost sheep, warning endangered cities and bearing abundant fruit. But none of the imagery seems to offer more instruction than that of fishing.

Right here, I might as well make a confession. I have *never* caught a fish. In 1975, after the fall of Vietnam, I helped 170 Vietnamese refugees on Guam launch a fishing company. Out of gratitude the men elected me—a non-fisherman—to be their company's "eternal president." I told them that with a president at the helm who had never caught a fish the company was doomed to fail. Sure enough, a year later, the company collapsed. But not because of the president! (All the fishermen chose to move on to the comforts of mainland United States.)

During that year of association with Vietnamese fishermen, I still never caught a fish. But I did learn some valuable lessons about fishing that clearly apply to the task of personal evangelism.

An evangelist, like a fisherman, must

- know what he or she is doing
- go where the fish are
- use the right bait
- think like a fish
- work hard
- be very patient
- believe there are hungry fish
- remember that fish are slippery
- not be content just to get his or her hook wet

To this list you could add a few similarities of your own. But there is also one very significant difference. When you catch fish, they are alive but they die; when you catch people, they are dead but they live!

There is no thrill, I am told, like the first catch. Although I have never had that thrill, I have experienced the thrill of catching people. Nothing can compare with the excitement of seeing dead men and women, youth and children come alive through faith in Jesus Christ!

From Mark's account of Christ's calling those first four disciples and from my personal experience of fishing for people in various parts of the world, I want to suggest four essential ingredients of any ministry for Christ that is to be fulfilling. They are example, enlistment, equipping and evangelism.

1. Example

"Come, follow me," Jesus said, "and I will make you fishers of men." (1:17)

From what precedes this call of Jesus to the fishermen, it is evident He was busy doing exactly what He was about to train them to do. Jesus set an example of evangelism, and then He called His disciples to evangelize.

As Peter, Andrew, James and John followed Christ Jesus during His remaining three years of ministry on earth, they saw Him evangelize everywhere He went. They watched as He witnessed to the Pharisee Nicodemus, the woman at the well, the lame man by the pool, Zaccheus in the tree, Levi at his tax booth. They heard what He said to the blind, the leprous, the deaf, the demon-possessed. Some years later, Luke, summing up Christ's earthly ministry, penned the words, "In my former book, . . . I wrote all that Jesus began to do and to teach" (Acts 1:1). Notice that Christ's deeds preceded His teaching. He demonstrated the lesson before He taught it. Thus modeling was a crucial step in His evangelism training.

Paul also applied this principle to his ministry. "Follow my example," he wrote to the Corinthian disciples, "as I follow the example of Christ" (1 Corinthians 11:1). "Join with others in following my example," he told the

Philippians. "Take note of those who live according to the pattern we gave you" (Philippians 3:17). He praised the Christians at Thessalonica: "You became imitators of us and of the Lord. . . . And so you became a model to all the believers in Macedonia and Achaia" (1 Thessalonians 1:6–7).

Paul passed along the same kind of advice to Timothy, his apprentice evangelist. "Don't let anyone look down on you because you are young, but set an example for the believers in speech, in life, in love, in faith and in purity" (1 Timothy 4:12).

Exemplary churches

In just three decades, Coral Ridge Presbyterian Church in Fort Lauderdale, Florida, grew from 17 to more than 7,000 members— and it is still growing! A chief factor in the church's amazing growth has been the example of the church's senior pastor, Dr. D. James Kennedy. Each week up to 500 people go out from the church to share the good news of Christ. Dr. Kennedy and his wife Anne set the pace. With such a large congregation to shepherd, a nationwide television ministry and scores of other demands on his time, Dr. Kennedy could justifiably delegate evangelism to others. But this evangelical leader knows the power of example.

At Christ Community Church in Omaha, I have observed the same power of example in our senior pastor, Rev. Robert L. Thune. He, too, will not delegate evangelism to his associates, elders or congregation. Every Thursday evening he participates in our Evangelism Explosion training, leading an evangelistic team of three out into the city.

All of the elders and deacons at Christ Community Church are trained in evangelism so they can be pacesetters for the congregation. Because of those examples, it is no surprise to see evangelism, church planting and missions given their proper biblical place in the church's priorities. And it is no wonder that the church has more than doubled in the past decade.

The importance of modeling cannot be emphasized enough. Whatever your position, you can set a good example in evangelism. Others may be waiting for your lead.

2. Enlistment

Another very crucial aspect of evangelism is evident in Jesus' encounter with the Galilean fishermen. That is *enlistment*.

> Without delay He called [James and John], and they left their father Zebedee in the boat with the hired men and followed him. (Mark 1:20)

Jesus enlisted James and John as His disciples, and they followed Him.

Jesus was busy evangelizing in Galilee. Before long He saw that He needed help. If His ministry of evangelism was to continue and expand, He must enlist helpers. In the next chapter of this book we are going to look at this matter of enlistment in greater detail. But let me just show you here how Jesus modeled for us the best way to enlist the people we are going to equip or prepare. He enlisted them prayerfully, privately and personally.

We are not specifically told that Jesus made the calling of Simon, Andrew, James and John a matter of prayer. But we do know that Jesus spent long hours in prayer to His Father. Just a little later Mark is telling us that "very early in the morning, while it was still dark, Jesus got up, left the house and went off to a solitary place, where he prayed" (1:35). Luke informs us that before Jesus selected from His disciples the 12 (including Simon, Andrew, James and John) who would be apostles, He "spent the night praying to God" (Luke 6:12). Prayer was a top priority on Jesus' agenda. Surely, then, prayer must have preceded the enlisting of those four fishermen.

Jesus instructed His disciples to enlist others prayerfully: "The harvest is plentiful but the workers are few. Ask the Lord of the harvest, therefore, to send out workers into his harvest field" (Matthew 9:37–38). We cannot, with human persuasion, motivate people to become involved in evangelism. God by His Spirit is the great Mover of people's hearts. So we go in prayer to Him and ask Him to do what we cannot.

Prayer is the first and most important step of enlistment.

A personal invitation

Next, Jesus contacted the four personally. He met them person-to-person on the shores of Galilee. He looked them in the eye and said, "Follow Me." There is no more effective way to enlist people for evangelism than by direct personal encounter. Your love, enthusiasm and concern add greatly to your invitation. Bulletin inserts, letters, phone calls, general announcements can also be used, but nothing gains a positive response like a personal encounter with people.

Jesus also enlisted privately. He did not preach a message on evangelism followed by an invitation for interested persons. He knew if He did that He would get the wrong volunteers, or that more would respond than He could effectively train. And so He sought privately the right people and the exact number He wanted. We will do well to follow His example.

In December, 1979, I candidated at Christ Community Church, Omaha, for the position of associate pastor for outreach. An inner core of leaders that I affectionately call the "Mafia" invited me out for lunch. Over lunch I spoke privately and personally to them about training for personal evangelism. Then I asked if I could take their picture.

"What for?" they wanted to know.

"Well, it will be six months before Donna and I return here, and we're going to pray daily for each of you that you will allow us to equip you for the task of evangelism that lies ahead!"

God answered our prayers. Upon our return to Omaha we began training the church treasurer, secretary, missionary treasurer, senior pastor's wife and office secretary. Gradually we enlisted and equipped each of the other church leaders. Then these leaders joined us in equipping our congregation. At this writing over 700 people in the church have been equipped to share the gospel with their friends, neighbors, family and associates.

3. Equipping

> "Come, follow me," Jesus said, "and I will make you fishers of men." At once [Simon and Andrew] left their nets and followed him.
>
> When he had gone a little farther, he saw James son of Zebedee and his brother John in a boat, preparing their nets. (Mark 1:17–19)

Note Jesus' statement, "I will make you," and the activity of James and John, "preparing their nets." When Jesus said, "I will make you fishers of men," how did He intend to do it? What method would He employ? Answer: The same way fishermen are trained to fish for fish. The same method Joseph used to train Jesus in carpentry. *Apprenticeship*—on-the-job training.

From childhood, Andrew, Peter, James and John had followed their fathers to the sea. They had watched their dads' every move. They had practiced under their dads' tutelage until they could reproduce to perfection the fishing skills of the older men.

Likewise Jesus, from the time He could barely toddle, had been an observer in Joseph's shop. He watched admiringly as His earthly "father" sawed and planed various sizes of lumber, later assembling them into tables and chairs that would be sanded, stained and polished. As Jesus grew, He developed through observation, instruction and practice the same skills.

Today people learn to fly an airplane that same way. At first they go up on a plane and watch the instructor fly it. Then the instructor will let them try some of the simpler motions, adding new abilities each lesson until the teacher feels they are ready to "solo."

Jesus taught His disciples to evangelize in this manner. First He demonstrated how it was done. Next He taught them basic truths and principles of the gospel. Then He sent them out to try their hand at fishing for men. When they reported back some of the difficulties they had encountered, He refined their skills. Finally He commissioned them to go and make disciples who, in turn, would be able also to make disciples.

Unfortunately, present day churches, Bible colleges and seminaries are trying to train evangelists in the classroom. It does not work. We must return to Christ's method of equipping.

They were "preparing their nets"

Regarding equipping, notice again that James and John were "preparing their nets." Other versions say "mending their nets." In Greek it is the same word Paul later uses to speak of the pastors and teachers who "prepare [equip] God's people for works of service" (Ephesians 4:11–12).

To carry the fishing metaphor a little further, I see the church as a giant net that Jesus Christ wants to cast over our cities, towns and hamlets. I like to define that net as a "bunch of nothings" tied together. Christ called simple, rugged, uneducated, smelly fishermen—the "nothings" of Galilee—to do His task of evangelism. In three years' time He knit them together, prepared them, "mended" them into a strong net that on a single day, to the glory of God, swelled the church from 120 to more than 3,000 people.

And Jesus intends that our churches today continue to serve as nets for gathering in the burgeoning populations around us. Why are they not doing so? Why are we not doing so? Because our nets are torn and shabby. They are no longer effective. They sorely need mending. The Christians need equipping. And according to Ephesians 4:11–12, equipping is the pastor's job. If your pastor-teacher is not preparing you for "works of service"—and what work of service has a higher priority than winning people to Christ?—let him know you expect him to do so.

It has been well said that if you catch a fish, you feed a man for a day. But if you train the man to fish, you feed him for a lifetime. For 20 years of my ministry I simply caught fish. I trained only a few others to do what I was doing—and that was more by accident than deliberate planning. Yes, I exhorted Christians to fish. I tried to explain to them how to fish. I exemplified fishing both in my preaching and in one-to-one encounters with people.

But then in 1977, in Hong Kong, I learned about a method—Evangelism Explosion—that enabled me to effectively train others for personal evangelism. Preparing others for works of service is no longer just a dream or a ministry ideal. It has become an exciting reality. I have seen hundreds of lay people, pastors, missionaries—even denominational administrators—trained to share with me in the marvelous task of fishing for men.

Jesus was a realist. When He commanded His

followers to make disciples of all nations, He knew it could happen. And He modeled for them a strategy to accomplish this worthy goal. If each of us, His followers today, will take His command seriously and follow His plan diligently, we will begin to see His objectives for evangelism achieved in our nation and around the world.

I never met a more friendly, winsome, outgoing, zealous Christian than Bill. Everywhere he went he made friends with people. And sooner or later he got around to sharing the gospel with them.

But one day he complained to me that very few if any of these friends to whom he witnessed ever came to Christ. He asked me to help him.

Naturally, I wanted to help Bill. But there was a problem. Bill attended another very fine church, and I did not want to pull him away from that fellowship. So I made him an offer.

"Bill," I said, "if you'll bring your pastor with you, I'll train you both, and then you can go back to your church and together train the rest of your congregation."

At the appointed day, Bill arrived with his pastor and six others from the congregation. For two semesters we prepared them and then sent them back to reproduce the training in their church. The pastor later took further leadership training at an Evangelism Explosion clinic. Today he has developed in his church a model ministry of equipping people for personal evangelism.

But the point I want to make is this: Bill continues to make friends and share Christ wherever he goes. But now there is a difference. Now he is seeing many of them respond with clear-cut commitments to Christ. That is because, at last, he has been equipped.

4. Evangelism

And so we return, following our look at the *example* of Jesus and His *enlistment* and *equipping* of disciples to *evangelism* itself—the actual purpose of these other considerations.

> Jesus went into Galilee, proclaiming the good news of God. "The time has come," he said. "The kingdom of God is near. Repent and believe the good news!" (Mark 1:14–15)

Jesus was proclaiming good news. He was an evangelist. And He intended that all who followed Him would become evangelists.

When He "saw Simon and his brother Andrew casting a net into the lake," He invited them to follow Him. "I will make you fishers of men," He promised (1:16–17). Jesus planned that those simple men who were casting a net into Galilee would thereafter cast evangelistic nets among the masses of people in the villages and cities where they lived and labored. Little did Simon Peter realize that three years later he and his colleagues would in one day pull in a net full of 3,000 people. Evangelism was a way of life for the early church. Every apostle, deacon, elder and rank-and-file Christian witnessed.

That phenomenon caused Elton Trueblood to say, "No one is really a Christian at all unless he is an evangelist or is getting ready to be one." It is a strong statement, but if we believe what we read in the New Testament, we must agree with it.

And yet it has been estimated that in our day about 95 percent of evangelical Christians have never led a person to Christ. What has happened? When did the church stop witnessing?

From church history we learn that for three centuries Christians continued to witness faithfully. But then a Christian Caesar—Constantine—gained the throne of the Roman Empire. In A.D. 313, Emperor Constantine issued the Edict of Toleration, effectively stopping the persecution of Christians. There were other edicts, too, including one that declared the entire Roman Empire Christian. Of course, if everyone was a Christian, evangelism was no longer necessary.

With a church full of people who were Christian in name only, responsibility for witnessing soon enough was relegated to the clergy. Unfortunately, that deplorable pattern, set in the fourth century, has been followed right down to our day.

But a new day is dawning! More and more Christians are realizing that it is their *privilege* as well as their responsibility to witness. More and more pastors are understanding that their task is not simply to do the work of an evangelist but to equip the Christians in their congregations to evangelize.

This is a good place to stop and ask exactly what evangelism is. Terry Wardle, in his book *One to One*, defines evangelism as "communicating the good news of salvation to men and women everywhere, giving them a valid opportunity to receive Jesus Christ as Lord and Savior and to become faithful, responsible members of His church."

That was what Jesus was doing—communicating good news. Our world is busy communicating news, but most of it is bad, very bad. My favorite cartoon series is Frank and Ernest. One day Frank was on duty to broadcast the five o'clock news. "I have good news and bad news tonight, folks," Frank announced. "And the good news is I'm not going to tell you the bad news!"

I saw some of the bad news while riding an airport limousine from Nyack, New York, to Newark, New Jersey. It was staring at me from the front-page headlines of the New York *Daily News*, lying between Felix, the driver, and me. I did not comment on the paper, but instead engaged Felix in friendly conversation about his family, job, interests and religious background.

He wanted some good news

Suddenly, somewhat embarrassed to see those ugly newspaper headlines, Felix remarked, "Pretty bad stuff, eh?" And then, half apologetically, "I wish they'd come out with some good news once in a while."

"Yeah, Felix," I agreed, pulling a New Testament out of my vest pocket. "And you know what? I just happen to have a little book full of the kind of good news you're looking for. Would you like me to share a bit of it with you?"

With Felix's consent I shared the gospel in considerable detail. I learned that several months previous he had received Christ while in the hospital, but he did not understand much about what had happened. One day after that, confused and frustrated, he had pulled his vehicle off the road and asked God to send him someone to explain it all more clearly.

When we pulled up to the air terminal, I prayed with Felix to confirm his earlier decision and gave him a Gospel of John and appropriate tracts. As he helped me unload my bags from the trunk, he thanked me profusely for sharing with him such wonderful, saving news.

To me, sharing the good news of Jesus Christ with a New Jersey chauffeur that day was every bit as exciting as announcing it for the first time to a village of tribespeople in Vietnam. I have noticed that people are usually more anxious to hear the gospel than we Christians are to share it.

But what does evangelism really accomplish? What happens when you and I share the good news? First, *it changes people*. It is "the power of God for the salvation of everyone who believes" (Romans 1:16). The gospel reaches down into the deepest recesses of the human heart and brings about a change so dynamic and dramatic that Paul compares the change to creation: "If anyone is in Christ, he is a new creation; the old has gone, the new has come" (2 Corinthians 5:17).

As my visitation team of three entered Carol's apartment and looked around at the pictures, the videos and the records, I said to myself (God forgive me!), *There's no way this gal's going to listen to us tonight. And if she does, there's just no chance of her coming to Christ.* Imagine my shock when she not only listened attentively but opened her heart to the gift of eternal life!

Carol began attending church regularly. She went through the new believer's class, joined the church, completed two semesters of evangelism training and became a beautiful, Spirit-filled Christian. One day my son John announced that he wanted to find a wife just like his mom. I gave him the names of three very attractive, godly girls in our church. Carol, as you may have already guessed, was one of them. Today it is difficult for me to believe that the Carol I met that first night is the Carol who now sits with my son John at our table for family Sunday dinner. Yes, evangelism changes sinners.

But evangelism also *changes Christians*. When a believer begins to take seriously the Lord's command to make disciples, when he or she begins to obey the Lord by faithfully sharing the gospel, God the Holy Spirit fills that person's life. Peter testified to this fact: "We are witnesses of these things, and so is the Holy Spirit, whom God has given to those who obey him" (Acts 5:32).

Paul wrote to a fellow believer: "I pray that you may be active in sharing your faith, so that you will have a full understanding of every good thing we have in Christ" (Philemon 6). When believers begin taking personally this matter of witnessing, they are not only filled with the Holy Spirit, but the gifts of the Spirit become more and more evident in their lives and ministries.

Conservative Baptist missionaries Al and Carol were among the first to be trained for evangelism at our church in Hong Kong. At the end of the first semester of training, Al came to me and said, "What have you done to Carol?"

"I don't know what you're referring to, Al," I replied.

"Tom, haven't you noticed? She's a different person. She used to be shy and somewhat withdrawn. But since she's become involved in this training, she has a new boldness, a new grace and a new desire to reach out to people. I can't believe the change that's come over her!"

Yes, evangelism changes Christians.

It changes churches, too

And because it changes Christians, evangelism also *changes churches*. When Christ was on earth in His physical body, He was constantly evangelizing. And when the Holy Spirit came upon the believers at Pentecost, they all began to witness. That is God's model for a healthy church.

We might say that a church to be a church in the New Testament sense must be an evangelizing church. It is not enough for a church to be "evangelical"—*holding* to the truth of the gospel. A church must also be "evangelistic"—that is, *sharing* the gospel with a non-Christian world.

While traveling through Israel some years ago, I saw two seas that reminded me of two kinds of churches. First, I visited the Dead Sea. There was no sign of life anywhere: no trees, no grass, no birds, no fish and, as far as I could see, no people. Later I stood on the banks of the Sea of Galilee. It was bursting with life! Everything was green. Birds were everywhere. Fishermen were pulling in large catches of fish from their nets. People were enjoying a happy life on its shores.

The difference is well-known. The Dead Sea has water flowing into it, but none flows out. The Sea of Galilee receives and discharges water at approximately the same rate. The Sea of Galilee symbolizes the New Testament church. The Dead Sea symbolizes a church that receives abundant blessing from the Lord but does not pass it on to a parched world.

Both in Hong Kong and Omaha, I have been privileged to be a part of churches that, like the Sea of Galilee, overflowed through aggressive evangelism. And in both cases I have seen how evangelism changes churches. With the steady addition of new believers comes an unmistakable vitality. The worship times reflect it. The churches become more visitor-friendly. Money is no longer tight. Missionary vision and enthusiasm increase. Instead of interpersonal feuds, members focus on the needs of others. Love and unity prevail.

That is what happens when a church decides to make Christ's last command its first concern. The Holy Spirit, in response to the church's obedience, takes control, distributing His gifts and producing His fruit. And when the Spirit of God is in control, Christ is lifted up. The church grows spiritually, numerically and organizationally. God is glorified.

Yes, evangelism changes sinners, saints and churches.

There is nothing quite as fulfilling as fishing for people and training others to do the same!

Are you fishing for people? If not, you may not be truly following Jesus. If you are fishing for people, are you also equipping others to do the same?

Jesus exemplified evangelism. He enlisted personal evangelists. He equipped those He enlisted. Together they evangelized. Jesus' methods are practical and proven; they work.

Try them and see for yourself.

Study Questions

Mark 1

1. List some of the metaphors the Bible uses for evangelism.
2. List some of the similarities between fishing and evangelizing, then some of the differences.
3. What does it mean to you to really "follow" Jesus? What does Jesus imply you will be doing if you really are following Him?
4. Who is the best example you know of someone who is "fishing for men"? What made you think of that person?
5. How does your church enlist and equip people for evangelism?
6. If you were to die today and stand before heaven's gate and God were to ask you, "How

many people have you brought with you to heaven?" what would you say?

7. If He were to ask you, "How many soul-winners have you personally trained while on earth?" what would you say?

CHAPTER 3

Extending Christ's Kingdom

Acts 1

SHORTLY AFTER THE DEATH of Chairman Mao Tse-tung, the Chinese Communist Party announced it would respect the "last wishes" of its deceased chairman by continuing his policies both at home and abroad. "The thoughts of Mao Tse-tung will always guide us in our forward progress," the party declared in a front-page news story carried by the *People's Daily*.

In methodology copied by Chairman Mao, Jesus Christ gathered from the grass roots of first-century Jewish society a band of revolutionaries. He thoroughly indoctrinated them, giving them careful, on-the-job training to establish a new kingdom—the kingdom of God.

Alas! While the kingdom Jesus sought to establish was still in embryonic form, enemies
put its Founder to death. The dreams of Jesus'
disciples for a better, happier life died with the
death of their Leader.

But an incredible thing happened. Jesus, who
beyond all argument was dead, His body
spice-wrapped in burial cloth and sealed
within a guarded stone tomb, came back to life!
His disciples' hopes revived! Surely nothing
could now hinder the spread of Christ's
kingdom to the ends of the earth.

But Jesus' disciples were not yet ready to
promote a new kingdom. They needed some
further instruction.

> After [Jesus'] suffering, he showed him-
> self to [his chosen apostles] and gave many
> convincing proofs that he was alive. He
> appeared to them over a period of forty
> days and spoke about the kingdom of
> God. On one occasion, while he was eating
> with them, he gave them this command:
> "Do not leave Jerusalem, but wait for the
> gift my Father promised, which you have
> heard me speak about. For John baptized
> with water, but in a few days you will be
> baptized with the Holy Spirit."
>
> So when they met together, they asked
> him, "Lord, are you at this time going to
> restore the kingdom to Israel?"
>
> He said to them: "It is not for you to

know the times or dates the Father has set by his own authority. But you will receive power when the Holy Spirit comes on you; and you will be my witnesses in Jerusalem, and in all Judea and Samaria, and to the ends of the earth." (Acts 1:3–8)

In these last words of Jesus Christ while He was on earth, we discover His masterful plan for extending His kingdom to the ends of the earth. Jesus spoke in response to the disciples' question regarding the kingdom. When we scrutinize the disciples' question and Jesus' answer, it is fascinating to discover that actually there are five questions being asked by the disciples and five answers given by Jesus.

During the Vietnam war, one of the American generals said that before he went into battle he always asked himself and his troops five questions: What? When? How? Where? Who? Surely it was not coincidental that as Jesus readied His "troops" for battle, the same strategic questions came up. We want to examine Christ's last statement in light of those five questions.

1. What?

The question "What?" demands an explanation of the nature of a thing. Implied in the disciples' question was an inquiry into the nature of Christ's kingdom:

Lord, are you at this time going to restore the kingdom to Israel? (Acts 1:6)

The disciples had had three years of exposure to Christ's teaching and another 40 days of post-resurrection studies dealing specifically with the "kingdom of God" (see Acts 1:3). But they still thought of Christ's kingdom as earthly and in the land of Israel. They still hoped Christ would be King of Israel and they would be His vice-regents.

Jesus, however, was intent on establishing and extending not the kingdom of *Israel* but the kingdom of *God*. The nature of that kingdom had been spelled out clearly by the Lord. We are indebted to Luke for many of the details:

- Jesus would reign as King forever. (Luke 1:33)
- Jesus' kingdom would not be of this world. (4:5–8)
- The kingdom would be established and extended by proclaiming the good news of a Savior/Lord. (8:1; 9:1–6)
- The kingdom would be further extended through prayer. (11:1–2)
- Those who wanted to participate in Christ's kingdom were to give it priority over material things. (12:30–31)
- The kingdom would start small, like a mustard seed, but grow large like a mustard tree. (13:18–19)

- The kingdom would be hidden in people's hearts like yeast is hidden in dough. (12:20–21)
- People least expected would be in the kingdom; some expected to be there would not be. (13:28–30)
- The kingdom would not come outwardly; it would be internal. (7:20–21)
- The kingdom would have to be received with childlike humility and simple faith. (18:16–17)
- The rich would find entry difficult. (18:24–25)
- Those who forsook loved ones for its sake would be rewarded with eternal life. (18:29)
- Jesus would be entrusting to His disciples the means for the kingdom's extension. (19:11–13)
- Jesus would ultimately return as King, at that time rewarding His servants according to their faithfulness. (19:11–27)
- Signs would point to the time of Christ's return to set up His kingdom. (21:31)
- Those who served would be greatest in the kingdom. (22:24–30)

So *what* is the kingdom of God? Jesus taught that it is God's reigning through Christ in the hearts of those who hear and believe the gospel, receiving Jesus into their lives as Savior and Lord. It is spiritual, not political; divine, not human; at the present time internal, not external. It will grow and spread to the ends of the earth until Christ returns as King of kings to set up His outward, visible reign over the earth.

Could it be that believers today need a fresh understanding of what the kingdom of God really is? Is it possible that we, like the early disciples, seriously misunderstand the true nature of the kingdom of God? Are we deluded into supposing that the kingdom is church buildings, ecclesiastical organizations and the prestige and power attendant to them? Have we focused·our primary efforts on reforming society rather than transforming sinful hearts through the blood of Jesus Christ poured out at Calvary?

Is there an antidote for these tendencies? Yes. We must center our attention on the rule of Christ by His Spirit in our hearts and commit ourselves to extend that rule to the lives of people in our communities and in every nation on earth.

2. When?

The "When?" question obviously has to do with time. That was precisely what the disciples wanted to know:

> Lord, are you at this time going to restore the kingdom to Israel? (1:6)

For three years Christ's disciples had heard their Lord speak of His kingdom. Then they had watched His crucifixion. With His death, they had seen their kingdom hopes dashed. But now He had risen from the dead, conquering mankind's most universal and most feared enemy. What could stand in the way of His setting up a throne in Jerusalem and ushering in the long-awaited kingdom? We can almost detect impatience in their phrase "at this time."

Today we live in an age of similar restlessness. Instant coffee, fast foods, rapid transit, one-hour photo labs and speedways that offer, of all things, express lanes. We are terribly rushed. We want everything, including the kingdom, posthaste!

The inimitable A.W. Tozer, in *Renewed Day by Day*, has a devotional in which he asks, "Are we just going around and around—like a religious merry-go-round? Are we just holding on the painted mane of the painted horse, repeating a trip of very insignificant circles to a pleasing musical accompaniment?"

And what was Jesus' reply to His disciples' question? He told them,

> It is not for you to know the times or dates the Father has set by his own authority. (1:7)

Jesus replied, first, that God the Father had kept secret the schedule for crowning His Son

King of kings here on earth. But then He told them there was coming an event, the timing of which they could know and about which they should be concerned. That had to do with when the Holy Spirit would come on them. It was an event that earlier He had promised would take place "in a few days" (1:5).

How important it is that we know the Holy Spirit has come into our lives! That coming is not only at the time of our spiritual rebirth but subsequently and daily for victorious living and fruitful service.

Many wonderful blessings

When the Holy Spirit enters and we give Him control of our lives, He brings to us many wonderful blessings. Jesus promised His disciples,

> You will receive power when the Holy Spirit comes on you; and you will be my witnesses. (1:8)

This is extremely important to the extension of His kingdom, for without God's power, the disciples' witness would amount to nothing. The greatest untapped power in the world is not some Niagara, or the awesome power of a tornado or the power locked in an atom. It is the Spirit's power waiting to be released from our lives.

Certainly Jesus remembered how one of His

disciples, Peter, in a moment of self-confidence, had vowed to be Jesus' faithful witness. And how Peter, depending on his own limited resources and human resolution, miserably failed to witness to a young woman in the high priest's courtyard. What Peter needed now was a new power, the power of the Holy Spirit, to replace his crippling fear with courage and boldness. Only then would he be able to witness to Christ effectively.

Just as Jesus had promised, a few days later the Holy Spirit descended upon Peter. Something dramatic happened. Peter received power from God. Instead of the old fear of people, he was fearless. Empowered by the Holy Spirit, Peter and the other apostles witnessed with boldness and enthusiasm.

To witness without the Holy Spirit's power

To try to witness without the Holy Spirit's power is futile and fruitless. You may have an outgoing personality. You may be very articulate. You may be a born salesman. You may have mastered the latest communication skills. You may even have memorized a convincing gospel presentation. But without the power of the Holy Spirit, you are a pair of beautifully knit gloves without hands in them, a new sleek Cadillac whose gas tank is bone dry.

The divine enabling of God's Spirit is so essential to the extension of His kingdom that Jesus commanded His disciples,

Do not leave Jerusalem, but wait for the gift my Father promised. (1:4)

Yes, Jesus wanted His disciples to witness, but not until they had received the Spirit's enabling.

Dialogue is often proposed as the ideal way to share the good news. Dialogue involves both persons in evangelistic exchange. But for the Spirit-filled witness, dialogue becomes "tri-alogue." The dynamic participation of this Third Person in evangelism makes all the difference. The Holy Spirit gives the witness boldness, wisdom, love and clarity of expression. And to the sinner He brings conviction, illumination and faith.

In the Revelation we find a clear allusion to evangelistic "tri-alogue." Jesus is speaking, and He says,

> "I, Jesus, have sent my angel to give you this testimony for the churches. I am the Root and the Offspring of David, and the bright Morning Star."
> The Spirit and the bride say, "Come!" And let him who hears say, "Come!" Whoever is thirsty, let him come; and whoever wishes, let him take the free gift of the water of life (22:16–17).

Often I have sensed the Spirit's presence and power as I witnessed. I remember the time I was sharing the gospel with Henry. Suddenly my mind went blank, I was tongue-tied and nothing I said seemed to make sense. But when I came to the end of my presentation and invited Henry to trust Christ, to my great surprise he responded positively! As a part of Jesus' "bride," I had uttered a very faltering, "Come." But the Spirit made up for my inadequacy with His powerful "Come!"

3. How?

"How?" clearly is a question inquiring into the means or method by which something will be done. The disciples had asked Jesus,

> Lord, are you at this time going to restore the kingdom to Israel? (Acts 1:6)

It is apparent from their question regarding the extension of Christ's kingdom that the disciples totally misunderstood the method that Jesus would employ.

The word *restore* in this question carries the idea of going back to a former condition, of putting something back in place. The disciples assumed that Jesus would renew the old covenant with Israel, restore the temporal power of David's throne and return Israel to its golden age of world influence, power and glory. To do this Jesus would have to lead a revolution to break Caesar's power and to overthrow Herod's rule. How else could an earthly kingdom be restored?

But Jesus' response, in contrast, suggested a totally new method of advance. For three years He had been training His disciples in His new methodology, but they had not yet caught on. He had said it before and He says it again:

You will be my witnesses. (1:8)

The disciples were looking back to an old system; Jesus was establishing a new society. They were thinking revolution; He was thinking regeneration. They were readying themselves for war; He was equipping them for witness. They envisioned a kingdom extended by political means; He, a kingdom extended by proclaiming good news. They dreamed of ruling; Jesus modeled and trained for serving. They wanted openings on the executive board; Jesus was hoping for volunteer evangelists.

Does it sound familiar? Why is it so easy to find believers willing to serve on the governing board or executive committee and so hard to find those who will train for personal evangelism?

At Christ Community Church we have taken a few serious steps to correct this imbalance. First, we have decided to screen our elders by requiring them to take 16 weeks of evangelism training before they can serve as an elder. The first leadership training Christ offered was an on-the-job course in fishing for men. So we are following His pattern by equipping our church leaders to be personal evangelists in whatever context of life they find themselves. As such they have become outstanding examples to the rest of the congregation.

A second step we have taken is equally important. We have begun developing future ministers of evangelism. That is because this rare brand of pastor cannot be developed on a seminary campus. His heart for outreach and his skills are best cultivated in the context of a dynamic, growing church. Some of these potential staff evangelists are coming up from the grass-roots of our local evangelism training. Others have come to us from other districts to serve as outreach interns.

During a church growth seminar in Minneapolis, I had a question for Rev. Robert Orr, vice president of the American Church Growth Institute. "If you were senior pastor of a growing church you wanted to continue to grow, and you felt the need to add another pastor to your leadership team, what type of staff person would you select?"

His answer surprised me, but it should not have.

"Unquestionably," Dr. Orr responded, "I would start with a minister of evangelism." He went on to explain that the traditional approach calls for adding a minister of youth, Christian education or music. But such a strategy, he said, focuses on the internal needs of the congregation and produces little if any growth. The calling of a pastor for outreach, on the other hand, focuses on reaching out, adding to the body of Christ. All other things being equal, this produces growth.

Incidentally, in Omaha we have chosen to title our staff evangelist Associate Pastor for Outreach rather than Associate Pastor for Evangelism. The rationale? The word *outreach* is less threatening to the people he visits than *evangelism* would be. *Outreach* is also broader in scope. It can and should include such related ministries as visitor relations, discipling, church planting and missions.

Christ's method in the first century for extending His kingdom was witnessing. And it is still His strategy today. Witnessing by pastors, of course. But witnessing also by church lay leaders and by all the laity. That is the "How?"

4. Where?

There is a fourth matter related to the kingdom that Jesus clarified for His disciples. "Where?" is a question pertaining to the place or location of a future happening. For the disciples, the logical place for the kingdom to develop was in Palestine, Israel's Promised Land.

Note how they specified Israel in their question:

> Lord, are you at this time going to restore
> the kingdom to Israel? (1:6)

The disciples, like all good Jews, looked upon
their own people as specially favored. God had
made His covenant with their father Abraham.
He had promised that the throne of David
would continue. The Jews were God's chosen
people.

They forgot that God had also said to
Abraham, "I will make you into a great nation/
. . . and all peoples on earth/ will be blessed
through you" (Genesis 12:2–3).

They forgot that God had said through the
prophet Isaiah, "I . . . will make you/ to be . . .
a light for the Gentiles,/ . . . to release from the
dungeon those who sit in darkness" (Isaiah
42:6–7).

How did Jesus correct the defective vision of
His disciples? He told them,

> You will be my witnesses in Jerusalem,
> and in all Judea and Samaria, and to the
> ends of the earth. (1:8)

Yes, Jesus said, the kingdom will be established in Jerusalem and all Judea, but it must
extend also to the hated Samaritans and even
to the remotest parts of the "unclean" Gentile
world.

Jesus was emphasizing balance. The
disciples' witness then and ours today must

reach *both* our home base and the remotest corners of the earth.

I have been privileged to take the gospel to Stieng Montagnards in the jungles of Vietnam. I have been privileged as well to lead to Christ in Omaha an all-American girl, Carol, who has since become my much-loved daughter-in-law. Both efforts were important; both have been equally fulfilling.

Churches lack balance

When I came home in 1979 after 25 years of ministry overseas, my first assignment was to travel from church to church, reporting on my missionary work. In that deputation, one fact caught my attention. The majority of churches I visited were out of balance. Generous giving, faithful prayer and outstanding recruitment for world missions were everywhere evident. But evangelism at home was noticeably absent. Some churches could not report one conversion or baptism in an entire year.

I am happy to say that a decade later there is nationwide a concerted effort to correct that imbalance.

At the same time there are other churches in our land that report exceptional local evangelistic success and church growth. But when it comes to world evangelization, they are woefully lacking. Those churches also need to achieve a balance.

As we have equipped and mobilized our

leaders and congregation at Christ Community
Church in Omaha for evangelism, the people's
involvement has developed within them Great
Commission hearts. Their vision for overseas
missions has increased. Missionary giving has
multiplied. Their zeal for planting new churches here at home has also expanded. As our
youth have been equipped and involved in
witnessing to their peers, they have become excited about the possibility of taking the gospel
overseas. In the past 10 years the number of
missionary recruits from our church has more
than quadrupled!

5. Who?

That brings us to the fifth and last of the
disciples' questions. "Who?" is a question of involvement, of responsibility. The disciples
were concerned to discover who would be
"restoring" the kingdom of God. Judging from
their question, they assumed the responsibility
rested with Jesus.

> "Lord," [they asked], "are you . . . going to
> restore the kingdom?" (1:6)

Behind the disciples' question was their ob-
vious desire to shift the responsibility to Christ.
After all, had He not just risen from the dead?
Did not He have the power now to do
whatever he wanted?

Here is where much of today's evangelism breaks down. We want to wriggle out of our mandate by shifting the responsibility to God—or to someone else. First there is the conscious or unconscious tendency to say, "God, you are the all-powerful Sovereign who elects, calls and ultimately saves. I know you will save whomever you want in heaven!"

That was precisely the attitude of a group of pastors in Northamptonshire, England, in the late 18th century. Young lay-preacher/cobbler William Carey having read *The Last Voyage of Captain Cook*, had constructed and hung above his workbench a world map to which he tacked all the international information and statistics he could find. At a meeting of local ministers Carey proposed a unique discussion subject: the duty of Christians to attempt to spread the gospel among the heathen. One of the ministers at the meeting, replied, "Young man, sit down! When God pleases to convert the heathen, He will do it without your aid or mine."

Carey was undeterred

Thankfully, Carey was not deterred by the opposition. He and a few other Baptist ministers formed The Particular Baptist Society for Propagating the Gospel among the Heathen. Less than a year later—June 13, 1793—Carey and his family and one other adult sailed for India as the society's first missionaries.

The penchant for consigning to God our evangelistic responsibility is probably found in all of us to some extent and for one reason or another. Perhaps we tend to think that because God is all-powerful, all-knowing and all-loving, He can reach our neighbor or work associate far better than we.

It brings to mind an amusing but true incident that happened in the home of one of my friends in Vietnam. This friend's young son came home from school with homework in art. After several unsuccessful attempts at a satisfactory drawing, the boy prevailed upon his artistic father to help him. The next morning the youngster proudly left for school bearing his masterpiece. But, as you might guess, the misrepresentation did not fool the teacher. At the end of the school day a tearful boy returned home to show his father his grade: a big red zero!

Yes, of course the father could do a far better job. But the assignment was the boy's. The teacher wanted to see the boy's best effort. So it is with personal evangelism. God could save the world without our lifting a finger or saying a word. But He has assigned the responsibility to us. He, too, is looking for our best effort.

Frequently our inclination to "pass the buck" has as its object the church pastor. After all, is he not better trained? Does he not have more time? Is he not more experienced in sharing the gospel? But it is we who have the non-Chris-

tian contacts. We have the in-depth relationships with unsaved relatives, friends, neighbors and associates. Christ's command to
witness was for every believer. The early
church's secret of rapid growth was that every
believer took seriously Christ's evangelistic
mandate.

Probably the most serious evangelistic "cop-
out" of our day is the oft-repeated insistence
that "evangelism just isn't my gift." It is interesting, is it not, that the same person would not
think of dodging his or her obligation to contribute financially to the church by saying,
"Giving is not my gift." A mother and father
would never evade their duty to bring up their
children with the excuse, "I don't have the gift
of teaching."

It is our responsibility

A World War II story concerns an acute milk
shortage in a European city. A rural pastor
heard about the city's predicament and called
upon the farmers in his country village to
donate to the need. Each was to bring a pail of
milk and pour it into a large barrel at the village church.

When the last farmer had poured his pailful
into the barrel, the pastor gathered the farmers
for a brief ceremony of thanks. Cup in hand,
the grateful pastor went to the barrel to draw a
sample drink. But he gasped in surprise when
only clear water came from the spigot. The red-

faced farmers discovered that each had brought a pail of water, assuming that all the others would contribute milk!

That scenario is too often repeated among us evangelical Christians who have the good news about Jesus Christ. We assume the other person—the pastor, the evangelist, the Sunday school teacher, the deacon, the "gifted witness"—will do the evangelizing. One day we will stand red-faced before our Lord, ashamed because of our dereliction in fulfilling Christ's Great Commission.

"Lord, are you . . . going to restore the kingdom?" the disciples wanted to know. I can almost see Jesus pointing His finger in their direction as He responds. *"You"* . . . *"*You will be my witnesses in Jerusalem, and in all Judea and Samaria, and to the ends of the earth" (1:8).

There is no escaping the finger of our loving Lord. It points straight at you and me! The responsibility is ours! He has done His part. He has finished His work of purchasing our salvation with His own blood. He has established His kingdom in our hearts. Now He desires—no, He commands—that we extend that kingdom to others. But He does not expect us to do it by ourselves. He promises to energize us by His Spirit's power.

Will we continue to evade this urgent task which is so incumbent upon each of us? Or will we rise in faithful obedience to extend God's kingdom?

Benjamin Franklin said, "He who will restore to men the primitive principles of Christianity will alter the face of the world." Franklin may have spoken more truly than he knew. It is a powerful statement. Read it again and reflect on it.

You and I can impact both the world around us and the remotest corners of our globe if we will but apply those "primitive principles" set forth by Jesus, our King, 20 centuries ago. In doing so, we will discover a ministry fulfilling beyond our wildest dreams!

In the next chapters we will encounter and examine more of the "primitive principles of Christianity."

Study Questions

Acts 1

1. What are five ways that the disciples' idea of the kingdom differed from Jesus'?
2. How would *you* define Christ's kingdom?
3. When exactly does the Holy Spirit enter a believer's life? What is His relationship to witnessing?
4. In light of Peter's denial of Jesus, how do you account for his bold witness in the book of Acts?
5. If you were senior pastor of a church and

needed to add a second staff person, what would the focus of his ministry be?

6. When it comes to evangelism, how do you reconcile the sovereignty of God and the free will of man? In other words, if God elects people to His kingdom, why do we need to witness anyway?

CHAPTER 4

Mobilizing Inactive
Congregations

Acts 11

FOR THREE YEARS BRITISH Preacher Richard Baxter delivered from his pulpit polished sermons that were marked by zeal and authority. Yet he saw little result.

"Oh God," the discouraged minister prayed, "You must do something with these people or I will die!"

In response God seemed to say, "Baxter, you have put forth your best efforts in the wrong place. You have expected revival to come through the church. Now try the home!"

Baxter began systematically calling in the homes of his parish, spending entire evenings with families. Before long, revival fires burned brightly, spreading through the church to the community around.

Worship must lead to witness

Richard Baxter learned what we in today's church desperately need to learn: our worship must lead us to witness. If we want to impact our generation and our world for Christ, we must break out of the four walls of our sanctuaries. We must somehow creatively and lovingly take the good news of Jesus Christ to hurting, spiritually hungry families in our neighborhoods.

If our worship does not inspire us to evangelize our unsaved families, friends, neighbors and associates, we may question whether we have truly worshiped at all.

In Chapter 3 we considered Christ's final words to His apostles. He expected them to extend His kingdom from Jerusalem to all of Judea and Samaria, and to the ends of the earth (see Acts 1:8). Following Pentecost and the filling with the Holy Spirit, Jesus' followers and their converts evangelized Jerusalem. Prodded by persecution, they continued on to evangelize Judea and Samaria, establishing growing churches in these places.

But their strong Jewish prejudices restrained them from witnessing to the world of Gentiles beyond these essentially Semitic enclaves. There was at least one exception. Urged by the

Holy Spirit, Philip witnessed to an Ethiopian official—a proselyte to Judaism on his way back to East Africa—and through the Scriptures brought him to faith in Jesus Christ and baptized him (Acts 8:26–39). We will look at that phenomenal incident in Chapter 10.

Cornelius opened the door

It was, however, the events surrounding the conversion of Cornelius, the Roman centurion residing in Caesarea, that opened the Gentile world—the "ends of the earth"—to the witness of Jesus' followers.

Like the Ethiopian, Cornelius was a proselyte to Judaism. Although devout and God-fearing, he knew nothing of Christ the Savior. He still needed to hear the gospel. How would that happen? Would God send an angel to him? Yes and no. God did send an angel, but not to tell him the good news about Jesus Christ. Rather, God sent the angel to tell Cornelius where he could find help. Not too far away in the town of Joppa, a man named Simon Peter was equipped to share with him the way of salvation. Cornelius sent to Joppa for God's messenger.

What exactly was Peter doing at that time? He was praying (Acts 11:4). Every great evangelistic advance begins with prayer. In fact, the entire evangelistic thrust of the first century began in an upper room prayer meeting.

Thereafter, the church of Jesus Christ advanced to the ends of the earth on its knees. And if we today want to see God's anointing on our evangelistic efforts, we must preface them and undergird them with fervent prayer.

When the envoys from Cornelius arrived in Joppa, they found Peter engaged in a believer's most important, meaningful activity—the one for which he was created and recreated. They found him worshiping God. But Peter's time of prayer and worship would mean little if it did not motivate him to take the gospel to the Gentile world that even in its most zealous search for God was still helplessly and hopelessly outside God's kingdom.

Christians hesitate to witness

How sad it is that the sinner—Cornelius— was more anxious to find the man who could bring him help than was the man—Peter—to take that help to him. Unfortunately, times have not changed much. Many Christians hesitate to witness because they suppose sinners are disinterested. As I said before, if the truth were known, we would discover that more want to hear the gospel than those who want to share it.

What would it take to move Peter from his rooftop place of prayer in Joppa to Cornelius' home in Caesarea? I suggest three experiences—the same basic three experiences that it will take to move any of us from our places of worship to the place of witness. They are a *vision*, a *voice* and a *visit*.

1. A Vision

We shall begin with a look at the *vision*, the first of Peter's three experiences:

> I was in the city of Joppa praying, and in a trance I saw a vision. I saw something like a large sheet being let down from heaven by its four corners, and it came down to where I was. I looked into it and saw four-footed animals of the earth, wild beasts, reptiles, and birds of the air. (Acts 11:5–6)

The biblical word *vision* implies spiritual sensitivity to see what cannot be seen by ordinary eyes. God alone may be pleased to reveal His intentions to His servants through visions. Others may *see* or *dream*, but only those in tune with God and His purposes have visions. What we see or what we dream becomes a vision only when God enables us to see the world as He sees it.

Peter had a vision. God used a vision of rather weird animals to arrest Peter's attention. He wanted Peter to realize that he had been seeing Gentiles as unclean, unapproachable, soulless beasts. As the animals in the four-cornered sheet were let down from (and later pulled up to) heaven, so God intended Gentiles from the four corners of the earth to be cleansed by the precious blood of Jesus and made fit for heaven.

The application for today is clear. Too often we, like Peter, treat the people around us like unclean, soulless creatures. God wants us to see that these neighbors, clerks, work associates are precious. He loves them, Christ died for them and God wants to redeem them and make them a part of His heavenly kingdom.

Hopefully such a vision will move us out of our comfortable places of worship to witness in the homes of the "Corneliuses" near us. For God desires not just apostles of old but believers of every age to catch a vision of lost people needing the gospel.

On April 30, 1975, when South Vietnam fell to Communist armies from the north, Donna and I found ourselves cut off from the people among whom we had worked and witnessed for 20 fulfilling years. It looked as if our missionary career had suddenly ended. At that very discouraging moment in our lives we needed a fresh vision. Like Peter, we needed to see that there were other people for whom Christ had died and who God wanted added to His heavenly kingdom.

Hong Kong, and a new start

One year later we accepted a call to pastor an English-speaking Chinese congregation of about 60 people in Hong Kong. All around us we found crowds of people—millions of them. But I must confess that for some time they were to me much like Peter's soulless beasts. Going to God in prayer, I asked Him for a fresh vision of what He wanted Donna and me to do in Hong Kong.

I saw no four-cornered sheet full of "wild beasts, reptiles and birds." But with the eye of faith I saw a church being packed to overflowing with people whom our congregation would win to Christ through an aggressive ministry of evangelism. I saw our church becoming a center for training pastors, missionaries and lay leaders in evangelism. I saw our church becoming a launching pad for sending witnessing Christians into mainland China. And somehow God by His Spirit gave me the faith to believe that He, in His perfect way and timing, would bring to pass all that I envisioned.

"But," you say, "I'm not a pastor or a missionary. What does such a vision have to do with me?" Just this: I have met scores of lay Christians just like you who have a vision of how God wants them to witness to their world.

These Christians have seen their world as a series of concentric circles similar to those Jesus described to His apostles just before He returned to heaven (Acts 1:8). But instead of "Jerusalem, . . . Judea, . . . Samaria, . . . ends of the earth," their circles have been immediate family, relatives, friends, coworkers, tennis

partners, hair stylists, insurance agents, plum-
bers, grocery store clerks. They believe that
God has placed them at the center of such a
network of relationships for a purpose: to
reflect to them Jesus Christ and to share with
them the good news of His saving grace. They
understand that they may well be the only ones
so strategically positioned to give those in their
circle of relationships opportunity to hear and
respond to the gospel.

With that clear vision they have set out to
pray, to love, to live Christ and to become
equipped to share their faith. Then when God
presents them with the opportunity, they can
tactfully, lovingly introduce their friends one
by one to Christ.

Realistic, New Testament living

This is not idealistic thinking. It is realistic,
New Testament living. I am seeing it in increasing numbers of my fellow believers. As Christians today catch such a vision, they seem to
discover a whole new purpose for living. They
find a fulfillment and a joy beyond description.

What kind of a vision do you have? Is it
moving you out of your place of worship to a
ministry of effective, fruitful witness?

2. A Voice

Peter saw a vision. But that was not his only

rooftop experience that day in Joppa. He also heard a *voice*.

> Then I heard a voice telling me, "Get up, Peter. Kill and eat." (11:7)

How wonderfully our God communicates! Having conveyed by a vision to Peter His plan of evangelizing the Gentiles, He now clarifies and reinforces that plan by the voice of His Spirit. I want you to notice two important features of God's communication with Peter. It was *personal* and it was *persistent*.

God called Peter by name. "Get up, Peter." Did you know that God, who created the innumerable host of stars above our heads also calls each of them by name? "He determines the number of the stars/ and calls them each by name" (Psalm 147:4). Is it any wonder, then, that He knows each of us by name? Are you aware that at various times and in different ways He speaks personally to you and me? He speaks to us by the voice of His Spirit, prompting us to rise and get busy in the evangelistic task so close to His heart. Sometimes He speaks through people, sometimes through circumstances. Often He communicates to us through His Word, the Bible. And there are times when He reaches us through some other piece of writing.

It was through a book that God spoke to me in Hong Kong. After God had given me a

vision for our church in Hong Kong, I wrestled
for a whole year over how to get started. At
first, I preached evangelistic sermons every
communion Sunday, because it appeared more
people attended those services. But nothing
happened.

To make matters worse, at the end of our first
year, William W. Kerr, the area director from
our church headquarters in the United States,
visited Hong Kong.

"Tom," the director asked me over lunch,
"how many people have come to Christ this
past year?"

A fruitless record

With embarrassment showing on my face, I
formed my fingers in the shape of a zero.
"But," I added, "it wasn't for lack of prayer or
evangelistic preaching. It just seems that people
in Hong Kong are more resistant to the gospel
than the people among whom I ministered in
Vietnam."

Kindly, my overseer encouraged me not to
give up. God would bless in His own time.
What I did not know that noon hour was that a
fellow missionary, Buddy Gaines, of the Orien-
tal Missionary Society, had been praying for
three years that God would raise up a pastor to
launch the ministry of Evangelism Explosion in
Hong Kong. He had purchased 30 copies of Dr.
Kennedy's book *Evangelism Explosion*. He had
even tried to acquaint other missionaries with

that evangelism method. But the missionaries were not interested. They supposed Evangelism Explosion was just another made-in-America, high-pressure evangelistic gimmick to manipulate people against their wills into a decision. Totally discouraged, Gaines advertised his unused books for sale at cost. Still no one was interested.

Finally, grasping for any kind of help, I telephoned Buddy and asked him to sell me a copy. Before I had finished the introduction, I discovered in great amazement that Evangelism Explosion was not a canned, button-holing evangelistic gimmick. It was a very practical, thoroughly proven, local church-centered New Testament strategy for evangelism, discipleship and church growth. It was a marvelous tool that a pastor could use to equip his church leaders and congregation for friendship evangelism and discipleship. Because it was so biblical and flexible, I reasoned that "E.E." (as it has come to be nicknamed), with a little adaptation, could easily fit my church situation in Hong Kong.

As I look back now, the reading of that book and the implementation of that strategy in our Hong Kong church became a very significant turning point in my life and ministry.

"Surely not, Lord!"

But back to Peter and God's voice to him.

How did the apostle respond to God's personal prompting to evangelize the Gentiles? He came up with a first-class excuse! Hear him tell it:

> I replied, "Surely not, Lord! Nothing impure or unclean has ever entered my mouth." (11:8)

What a contradiction! In the same breath Peter said "No" to God and called Him "Lord." If we call God "Lord," we must be prepared to respond "Yes" to whatever He asks us to do. We must submit to His rule and direction in our lives.

But how often we are guilty of similar contradictions! In our worship services we sing, "I'll go where you want me to go, dear Lord." But when the voice of His Spirit prompts us to witness to our neighbor, we clam up. I have had people tell me they were too old to learn to witness. "If I were young again," they have said, "full of vitality and enthusiasm, I'd take the training and share my faith regularly."

When God personally prompted Shirley, a member of our church in Omaha, to witness, she had second thoughts whether at her age she would be adequate for the challenge. But she enrolled in our evangelism training and was placed on my team. For 16 weeks I watched Shirley develop into a lovely, effective witness. Then one Sunday morning during the closing hymn, she came down the middle aisle of the sanctuary arm in arm with a woman about her age.

"Pastor Tom," she said to me, "this is my neighbor. This past week she trusted Christ as her Savior. She is coming forward to give public testimony to her new faith."

I knew Shirley could become an instrument for leading others to Christ because when Christ saved her, He left her on earth—just as He has left you and me on earth—for that very purpose.

"It's not my gift"

There is another excuse frequently offered by Christians to justify their disobedience. "Evangelism," they say, "is just not my gift." I suppose persons who use that excuse assume that since God "gave some to be apostles, some to be prophets, some to be *evangelists* [emphasis mine], and some to be pastors and teachers" (Ephesians 4:11), He excuses all the rest of us from any evangelistic responsibility.

The truth of the matter is that God has commanded every Christian to witness. The biblical record in the Acts (note especially 8:1, 4) implies that *all* first-century Christians participated in proclaiming the good news of salvation. Non-biblical sources convey a similar impression. In other areas of service, we expect a man to be willing to set up chairs even if "serving" is not his gift. We expect a woman to show mercy if a child comes to her with a scratched knee, whether or not "showing mercy" is her special gift.

A careful inspection of Ephesians 4:11–12 reveals that God has given evangelists to the church not just to proclaim the good news themselves, but *to equip fellow believers to do the same.* Repeat: witnessing is for everyone.

For the first 20 years of my overseas ministry, I was very active personally as an evangelist. I had the desire to equip my fellow believers for evangelism, but I did not know how. I preached many sermons exhorting Christians to witness, but I could not go much beyond that. After those 20 years in evangelism, I am embarrassed to admit that, at most, I probably trained a handful of people to witness. And that was more by accident than any deliberate effort.

Then in 1977, in Hong Kong, I read Dr. James Kennedy's book that I referred to earlier. Later, I attended an Evangelism Explosion leadership training clinic at Coral Ridge Presbyterian Church in Fort Lauderdale, Florida, where Dr. Kennedy ministers. At last I was able to begin equipping fellow-believers to witness. And I discovered hundreds of believers who, although *not gifted* as evangelists, nevertheless when equipped, become effective, fruitful witnesses.

Not "Am I gifted?" but "Am I willing?"

The question, I have come to realize, is not,

"Am I gifted?" The question is, "Am I willing to be equipped to witness?"

Another prevalent reason many Christians, like Peter, say "No, Lord" to witnessing is they think they do not have time. Time is something all of us have an equal amount of per day. Whether you are Billy Graham, Chuck Swindoll, Elisabeth Elliot, John Doe or Mary Smith, you have the same number of minutes in an hour, the same number of hours in a day and the same number of days in a year. I find that even the busiest persons usually have time for the activities most important and enjoyable to them. They simply put those activities at the top of their priority list.

If we are honest with God and with ourselves, the issue for us is not time but priority. The real question is "How important is Christ's Great Commission to me? How great is my desire to see my lost relatives, friends and neighbors come to Christ?"

But the most subtle deterrent of all, the one that more than any other keeps Christians from sharing their faith is *fear*. The threat of the unknown causes the most zealous and articulate of us to be silent when deep in our hearts we really want to speak.

"What kind of a response will I receive?" we ask. "What questions will they raise? Suppose they are not interested?"

I confess that for years I wrestled with the problem of fear. To stand before a crowd of 500 or 5,000 was no problem for me. When I spoke, I had well-prepared notes. I knew exactly what I was going to say. Normally no one would interrupt me. Usually my audiences were interested and responsive. There were few unknown factors to pose a threat.

Fear paralyzed me

But when it came time to witness to my seatmate on an airplane or to enter someone's home for the first time for the purpose of witness, I was paralyzed by fear. Thus, when opportunities arose to share Christ with my friends and neighbors, I rationalized something like Peter: "Surely not, Lord. They're probably not interested. I don't think I should impose my faith on them."

But as I read Dr. Kennedy's book, as I received hands-on training at the E.E. clinic, as I refined those witnessing skills in the context of my own church's parish, I watched that crippling enemy called "fear" weaken and vanish. With the aid of God's Spirit, I have a new liberty and delight in sharing the gospel with individuals for whom I have prayed for years. And through the E.E. equipping ministry I have seen hundreds of other people overcome their fears.

God spoke to Peter personally. He also spoke *persistently.*

The voice spoke from heaven a second

time, . . . This happened three times. (Acts
11:9–10)

When Peter raised excuses for not going to
Cornelius, the Roman soldier, God did not give
up on him. Persistently, patiently God kept
after Peter. And He does so today. When we
respond to God's evangelistic promptings with
our plethora of weak excuses, God does not
abandon us. Rather, He keeps knocking, calling, urging us to get busy in His whitened harvest field.

Are *you* listening to God's voice? Have *you*
obeyed His personal, persistent call? Or are
you, like Peter, continuing to answer, "Surely
not, Lord!"?

3. A Visit

The third experience God used to move Peter
from worshiping to witnessing was a *visit*.
Peter goes on to say,

> Right then three men who had been sent to
> me from Caesarea stopped at the house
> where I was staying. (Acts 11:11)

Actually, Peter mentions three visits: the visit
of the men sent from Caesarea, Peter's own
visit to the house of Cornelius and the visit of
the Holy Spirit as He descended upon those

who had gathered in Cornelius' house. We will look at the three visits in that order.

The men from Caesarea came to visit Peter at his place of prayer and worship. They were in search of saving truth. Every church that is worth its name has visitors. Many of these visitors, like the three men from Caesarea, are searching for God and His saving truth. But how are these visitors being treated?

In Acts 10, the chapter where this amazing account of Peter and the visitors from Caesarea is first told, we learn that the Holy Spirit said to Peter, "Get up and go downstairs. . . . I have sent [these visitors]. . . ." Then Peter invited the men into the house to be his *guests*. (10:20–23)

Too many churches treat visitors like strangers. Peter made these visitors his guests. How can we help the visitors to our church feel like guests?

One practical suggestion comes to mind. We can meet their parking needs. How many times I have visited churches and found all the choice parking places either reserved or taken. Senior Pastor Robert Thune at our church has set a good example by parking in a spot farthest from the church entrance.

Visitors also feel like guests when they are welcomed at the entrance by well-trained, friendly greeters. They will appreciate a welcome center that offers them helpful information about the church and signs in the foyer that direct them to their chief places of interest.

They are impressed by courteous, cheerful ushers who seat them properly. While they may be warmed by a general word of welcome during announcement time, they especially like *not* being singled out or asked to stand and introduce themselves. And even if they are disinclined to accept, they will appreciate being invited to an after-service visitor reception, or, better yet, a meal and a time of fellowship at the home of a hospitable member.

First impressions are lasting impressions. First-time visitors who are made to feel at home at your church will later be open to a meaningful personal witness to Christ's saving power.

Peter's visit to Cornelius

The second of the three visits was Peter's—as he was led by the three emissaries to Caesarea and the home of Cornelius, the Roman centurion.

> The Spirit told me to have no hesitation about going with them. (Acts 11:12)

The three men who had come to Peter came at the bidding of Cornelius, who in turn had received his instructions from an angel sent by God (10:3–6). The Holy Spirit, who had masterminded the entire scenario, assured Peter that he should go without hesitancy.

But notice something else that I consider significant: Peter did not make his visit alone. He took along "some of the brothers from Joppa" (10:23)—six in number. Peter in relating the story says:

> These six brothers also went with me, and we entered [Cornelius'] house. (Acts 11:12)

If at all possible, evangelistic calling should not be done alone. Jesus took with Him His 12 disciples. When He sent them out in ministry, He sent them two by two. Paul normally had associates with him—people such as Barnabas, Silas, Timothy, Titus—sometimes for the purpose of giving them on-the-job training. Peter, on his visit to Cornelius, took with him six of his Christian brothers.

When I read *Evangelism Explosion* in Hong Kong, I found an incredibly simple but effective strategy for following up church visitors. But I found more. I found also a biblical method for equipping lay people for evangelism through on-the-job training just like Peter did in the first century.

God used Kennedy's book and that strategy to help me move our Kowloon congregation out of our place of worship and into the community in effective, fruitful witness.

After I read the book, I loaned it to Doug Jensen, a young graduate of Wheaton College, who was in Hong Kong with his wife, Jodi, serving for one year as our pastor for youth.

The book so excited Doug that he stayed up all night reading it. The next morning he came to me full of enthusiasm.

"When do we get started?" Doug wanted to know.

"How about now?"

"How about tonight at seven?" I responded.

I invited one of our English-speaking members to join Doug and me. Although I had read *Evangelism Explosion*, not all of its details had yet registered in my mind. Otherwise, I would have chosen a woman, and not another man, to be the third member of our visitation team.

Looking over our church visitor list, I selected the name of Joyce, a Cathay Pacific Air Lines flight attendant. I called her for an appointment. She would be glad to see us.

That evening, without training, without experience, we three men walked into Joyce's apartment at the appointed hour. We took plenty of time becoming acquainted with this Indonesian-born woman, learning the details of her secular life, her religious background and her impressions of our church. Then, following as best I could the instructions in *Evangelism Explosion*, I shared my own testimony with her and asked her the first of two very searching questions:

"Joyce, do you know for certain that if you were to die tonight that you would go to be with God in heaven?"

"I hope so," Joyce responded somewhat un-
certainly. I followed up with question number
two:

"Joyce, suppose you were to die and stand
before heaven's gate, and God were to say to
you, 'Joyce, why should I let you into My
heaven?' What would you say?"

"I've gone to church," Joyce began. "I've
sung in the choir. I've lived a good moral life,
doing the best I can."

I told Joyce that we had some wonderful
news for her and asked if we might share it
with her. She got her Indonesian Bible in order
to read in her mother tongue the Scriptures we
quoted. When we came to the end of the gospel
presentation, I asked Joyce if she would like to
receive God's gift of eternal life.

The answer was "Yes"

"Yes!" she responded immediately, to our
great surprise and delight. Joyce began attending our church regularly. And shortly after
that, we returned and led her roommate to
Christ.

Extremely pleased with this new-found
strategy, I asked missionary Buddy Gaines,
who had sold me the book, to help me launch
the E.E. ministry in our church. Buddy agreed
to help me two evenings a week training two
teams of our church people. But because I was
the pastor, Buddy insisted that I teach the
material.

We started small with eight participants. In the first 16-week semester we saw 40 people turn to Christ through our in-training witness. Thirty-five of the 40 became a part of our Kowloon Tong Alliance Church. The next semester 40 more people put their trust in Christ, about the same percentage being added to the church.

Midway through the first semester I flew to Fort Lauderdale for leadership training at the place where it all had started. And then we organized our own leadership training clinic for Hong Kong pastors and missionaries. Enthusiasm and interest spread, spilling over to neighboring Asian countries.

In three years, our church grew from some 60 members to 350. And the ministry of E.E. spread all over Asia. Evangelism Explosion proved to be a New Testament strategy that helped the Kowloon Tong Alliance Church and me discover a ministry fulfilling beyond our wildest dreams.

But now we need to look at the third visit referred to by Peter. After the visit of the three emissaries to the house where Peter was worshiping, and during Peter's visit to the house of Cornelius in Caesarea, there was a visit by the Holy Spirit. Peter reports,

> As I began to speak, the Holy Spirit came on them as He had come on us at the beginning. (11:15)

This was the most important visit of all! Without the divine enabling of God's Spirit, Peter's witness would have been a failure. The Spirit brought power, boldness and love to Peter's witness. And He brought conviction, repentance and faith to Cornelius and his household.

How important it is for us, when we witness for Christ, to know that we cannot witness by dialogue alone. Let me say again that our witness must become a "tri-alogue" with the Holy Spirit included in the communication of the good news.

John the apostle writes, "The Spirit and the bride say, 'Come!' And let him who hears say, 'Come!' Whoever is thirsty, let him come; and whoever wishes, let him take the free gift of the water of life" (Revelation 22:17). The Holy Spirit joins with Christ's bride—the church—to woo and win sinners, inviting them to receive the gift of eternal life.

How often in sharing the good news I have seen the Holy Spirit do what I could not myself do. He has taken my faltering, inadequate evangelistic efforts and worked the divine miracle of regeneration in hearts that I could never hope to change.

An interdependence

There is a beautiful interdependence between the evangelist and the Holy Spirit. Without the other, neither could work and nothing would happen. The Holy Spirit needed Peter's witness, and Peter depended upon the Holy Spirit's work to bring Cornelius and his family into the household of faith. The Spirit needed the bride and the bride depended upon the Spirit.

There you have it: the *vision*, the *voice*, the *visit*. That was what it took to get Peter from his place of worship to God's place of witness. That is what it took for English Pastor Richard Baxter to see God bring new life to his church and community. And that is what it took to transform a discouraged congregation in Hong Kong into a vibrant, growing church whose witness impacted hundreds of people in Hong Kong and spread to other Asian lands.

How is your vision? Are you heeding the voice of the Spirit? Have you been involved in the three visits Peter experienced? Or are you still locked within the four walls of your church sanctuary?

God longs to see inactive congregations mobilized for unparalleled advance and growth. He desires to see you and the congregation with whom you worship effectively taking the good news to your community and to the most remote corners of earth. Those first century events that Peter reported in Acts 11 can be repeated in this era—in your life and in the lives of your fellow church members!

Study Questions

Acts 11

1. What was the cultural barrier (excuse) keeping Peter and the other disciples from taking the gospel to the Gentiles? What did God do to remove that barrier?

2. What are some of the barriers or excuses that keep Christians from witnessing today?

3. In light of Peter's culture, how might he have felt when the three persons sent out by Cornelius showed up at his door?

4. In light of this story, what do you feel is the destiny of very devout people with whom no one has ever shared the gospel?

5. Of what importance was the ministry of the Holy Spirit in this story? How does that apply to us today?

6. How would you define "vision"? Is it possible for lay people to have an evangelistic vision? Please elaborate why, and if so, how.

7. What would you say to someone who says, "I just don't have TIME for evangelism or to be trained to share my faith."

8. What do you see as the major causes of fear that people experience when it comes to evangelism, and how are such fears best overcome?

9. What does your church do to reach out to visitors? How might your visitor relationships be improved?

CHAPTER 5

Bearing Abundant Fruit

John 15

GOD LOVES FRUIT! WHEN He created fruit on day three, "God saw that it was good" (Genesis 1:12). God also loves *abundant* fruit. The "trees [bore] fruit with seed in it" so that the fruit could multiply. God was not satisfied with simple addition. He provided for multiplication. In His first command to mankind God said, "Be fruitful and increase in number; fill the earth" (1:28).

In the spiritual realm, God's desire also is that we bear abundant, abiding fruit. Thankfully, we are not left to guess how this can be accomplished. During His years of ministry on earth, our Lord Jesus drew many spiritual lessons from the abundant fruit trees and vines that He saw all around Him in Palestine. In what has come to be called His "Upper Room Discourse" (John 14–16), Jesus tells us just how we can become fruitful Christians.

It is important that we understand the context of what Jesus said to His disciples in that Jerusalem "upper room." Passover was approaching. Jesus was aware that His public ministry to the Jews was over. He knew that the time for His supreme work—His atoning death on the cross—had come. So He assembled His disciples for some very important instructions regarding His betrayal and death, His departure to prepare a place for them in heaven and the sending of the Holy Spirit. In this chapter we shall concentrate on what Jesus said about fruit bearing as John has recorded it for us. Jesus begins with the words:

> I am the true vine, and my Father is the gardener. (John 15:1)

Some commentators suggest that Jesus may have needed to look no farther than out of the windows of that upper room to see a grape arbor loaded with fruit. It would have been very natural for Him to point to it as He likened Himself to the vine and God the Father as the One who cared for it.

Israel likened to a grape vine

The nation Israel had frequently been likened to a grape vine. In fact, grape vines had become a symbol of the nation, the emblem on Maccabean-period coins, the decoration on the front of the sacred Jerusalem temple. Old Testament references, however, described Israel as a degenerate vine that, instead of "good" grapes, "yielded only bad fruit" (Isaiah 5:2).

How appropriate, then, that Jesus should announce that He, in contrast to the wild, degenerate vine that marked Israel, was the true Vine, and that His disciples, joined to Him by faith, were the branches. In union with Jesus Christ, they were about to emerge as the new Israel that would bring forth abundant, abiding fruit—good fruit—to the glory of God. Over and over, Jesus repeats the phrase, "in me":

Remain in me. (John 15:4)

If a man remains in me . . . he will bear much fruit. (15:5)

If anyone does not remain in me, he is like a branch that is thrown away and . . . burned. (15:6)

If you remain in me and my words remain in you, ask whatever you wish. (15:7)

Jesus wanted to make it very clear to His disciples that bearing abundant, abiding fruit could only take place as they remained attached to the trunk.

For many years Dick, together with his wife and children, had attended a strong evangelical church. He sang the hymns. He participated in the reading of the Scriptures. He even ushered. Everyone assumed Dick was a believer. But his life evidenced no assurance of salvation and no spiritual fruit.

Dick began attending our church with his family, but his barren, spiritually dead condition persisted. Then out of curiosity he signed up for our evangelism and discipleship training. As the weeks passed, Dick became uneasy. He was especially uneasy when the assignment called for him to write out his testimony. At last it became clear: he had not ever really trusted Christ for salvation!

Dick invited Christ into his heart. Almost immediately he evidenced new life and fruitfulness. He began sharing the gospel with many of his work associates, leading a number of them to Christ. From the time Dick became "joined" to Jesus Christ, the true Vine, he was a dynamic, fruitful Christian.

1. His Pruning

Being a lover of fruit, one of the first things I did when we bought our home in Omaha was to plant a number of fruit trees in our back yard. I even tried my hand at grapes! One thing about grape vines has become very evident to me: they require much attention! They must be watered, fertilized, sprayed, cultivated. The branches must be tied up, the birds kept away. Most of all, grave vines need to be pruned. Jesus speaks of that pruning:

> I am the true vine, and my Father is the gardener. He cuts off every branch in me that bears no fruit, while every branch that does bear fruit he prunes so that it will be even more fruitful. (John 15:1–2)

W. Phillip Keller in his book *A Shepherd Looks at Psalm 23* observes that sheep, of all domestic animals, require the most care. It is interesting that God likens us Christians to sheep and to the branches of grape vines, both of which need extreme amounts of care!

In Jesus' statement quoted above, our Lord underscores two kinds of care that must be given the branches by His Father, the Gardener: (1) those that are fruitless must be cut off and (2) those that are fruitful must be pruned.

Fruitless branches are cut off

First, about the *fruitless branches* that must be *cut off*. I used to have a problem with Jesus' statement about cutting off the fruitless branches. But then I looked a little farther to where Jesus says that those who "bear much fruit" are "showing [them]selves to be [His] disciples" (15:8). By contrast, the non-fruit-bearing branches are not Jesus' disciples. Their fruitlessness is proof of the fact. They may say, "Lord, Lord" (Matthew 7:21), but that does not signify they are a part of the kingdom. They are unregenerated followers of Christ, and Jesus will say, "I never knew you. Away from me, you evildoers!" (7:23). Commenting on these fruitless branches Jesus says,

> If anyone does not remain in me, he is like a branch that is thrown away and withers; such branches are picked up, thrown into the fire and burned. (John 15:6)

In another metaphor, Jesus calls these unregenerated followers "weeds [sowed] among the wheat" (Matthew 13:25). Jesus likened the kingdom of heaven to a field where wheat and weeds grew up together. But at harvest time, the weeds were separated from the wheat and, like the unfruitful branches, thrown into the fire.

While both wheat and weeds were growing, the weeds could not be clearly distinguished from the wheat. In the end, the weeds had a distinguishing mark: they bore no fruit! In explaining the parable to His disciples, Jesus called the fruitless weeds "the sons of the evil one" (13:38).

The inference of Jesus' parable is transparent. In the church there tend to be both believers and unbelievers. They may look alike. They sit in the same pews. They sing the same hymns. They bow their heads together at prayer time. They place their gifts in the offering basket. But at the end of the age they can be distinguished by whether or not they are bearing fruit. On that basis they will be rewarded or punished.

Jesus' parable of the man sowing seed on four kinds of soil (Matthew 13:1–23) teaches the same truth. The person represented by the "good soil" is the one who "produces a crop, yielding a hundred, sixty or thirty times what was sown" (13:23). Again, fruitfulness distinguishes the good from the bad.

Judas Iscariot, who had been sitting with the other disciples in the upper room as Jesus spoke of the vine and branches, only a few hours later proved to be one such fruitless branch. For three years Judas had appeared to be one of Christ's disciples. He had witnessed Jesus' miracles, had heard His teachings, had served as treasurer for the group. He had even shared in the Last Supper. But Jesus referred to this fruitless man as "the one doomed to destruction" (John 17:12). What a warning this should be to us to examine ourselves!

Fruit-bearing branches are cleaned up

Second, Jesus speaks of *cleaning up* the *fruitful branches*. The divine Gardener will prune "every branch that does bear fruit . . . so that it will be even more fruitful" (15:2).

Every branch as it grows gathers leaves and

runners that need to be pruned. Otherwise, the strength of the vine goes into those extraneous appendages rather than into the grapes. The skilled gardener knows how and when to remove those obstructions to the one purpose of the vine: fruit bearing.

For us as believers attached to Jesus Christ, the pruning is not done with knife but with the Word of Christ. Jesus says,

> You are already clean because of the word I have spoken to you. (15:3)

God the Gardener, through His Word, prunes from our lives those attitudes, motives, thoughts, words and actions that hinder fruitfulness. Jesus says,

> If you remain in me and my words remain in you, ask whatever you wish, and it will be given you. This is to my Father's glory, that you bear much fruit. (15:7–8)

He goes on to say,

> If you obey my commands, you will remain in my love, just as I have obeyed my Father's commands and remain in his love. (15:10)

One of the most fruitful, growing Christians I have ever known is a Korean businessman, C.

H. Koo, whom I had the joy of leading to Christ in Hong Kong. The first Sunday after he received Christ into his life, I happened to preach a message on the subject of fellowship. Mr. Koo took this message from the Word very seriously and called me the next day to invite Donna and me to his home for dinner. He said he wanted to begin having church people over every Friday evening for fellowship. He was starting with us.

What are you doing in Genesis?

The next Sunday I preached on the importance of spending time in God's Word. I suggested that if a person would read three chapters a day and five on Sunday, he could completely read the entire Bible in a year. Later in the week Mr. Koo called to ask me some questions about Genesis. I inquired what he was doing in Genesis.

"I'm starting on the three chapters a day you suggested to us last Sunday," he replied.

Whether the subject was tithing, prayer, witnessing or reaching out in love to other believers, dear Mr. Koo was diligently doing everything he could to obey God's Word and to allow it to bear fruit in his life. It was no wonder that he grew so rapidly. It was no wonder he soon became one of the most fruitful Christians I have known.

How is it in your life? Does the pruning knife need to trim away time-consuming activities that hinder your fruitfulness? What about those seemingly harmless items on your agenda that keep you from investing your best energies in bearing abundant fruit? Do you get carried away with overwork or too much recreation or unprofitable TV viewing? Why not submit your life right now to the Word of God for God's loving ministry of pruning?

Another pruning instrument

Besides the Word that Jesus speaks, another pruning instrument that God uses in our lives is the cross. Two or three days before His upper room discourse, as Jesus reflected on His coming death by crucifixion, He spoke a significant secret of abundant fruitfulness:

> I tell you the truth, unless a kernel of wheat falls to the ground and dies, it remains only a single seed. But if it dies, it produces many seeds. (John 12:24)

The principle of death, burial and resurrection is vital to abundant fruit-bearing. Sometimes, as with Stephen, the first Christian martyr, it is a literal death (Acts 6:8–14; 7:54–8:4). Sometimes the death is figurative—a "count[ing]" of ourselves as dead (Romans 6:3–11; Galatians 2:20). Let me illustrate them both out of personal experience.

For 20 years my sister Ruth and her husband, Ed Thompson, were missionaries in Kampuchea (Cambodia), in Southeast Asia. The people were unresponsive to the gospel; in all their years in Kampuchea, this very gifted and committed couple had only a handful of converts and a very small, struggling church in Kratie to show for their efforts. Then Prince Sihanouk expelled all Americans from his country, and Ed and Ruth moved across the border into Vietnam. They took up work among one of the highlands tribes, making their home in Banmethuot.

When the 1968 Communist Tet offensive occurred, Ed and Ruth realized their house was in the direct line of enemy fire. For safety they climbed down into their backyard bunker. As the fighting broke out, Ruth Wilting, a missionary nurse living in Banmethuot, ran to the Thompsons' bunker for shelter. A Communist soldier followed her, spraying the bunker with his automatic weapon. For good measure, he tossed in a hand grenade. All three missionaries were killed.

Like kernels of wheat

The bodies of Ed and Ruth Thompson and Ruth Wilting were never moved. Like kernels of wheat, they fell into the ground and died.

On the first anniversary of their death, I flew to Banmethuot to place on the grave site three marble markers engraved with Christ's promise: "Unless a kernel of wheat falls to the ground and dies, it remains only a single seed.

But if it dies, it produces many seeds" (John 12:24). And in the years that have followed, I am glad to report that from that bunker grave has come an abundant harvest, just as Jesus predicted.

Our daughter Jennifer, when she heard the sad news of her aunt and uncle's deaths, was moved to trust Christ as her Savior and Lord. Ed and Ruth's sacrifice was the catalyst for others across the United States and Canada to receive Christ into their lives. Still others committed themselves to serve as missionaries.

Across the Vietnam border, a large number of Kampucheans, unresponsive when Ed and Ruth proclaimed the gospel among them, upon news of their violent end, turned in faith to Jesus Christ. In their deaths, Ed and Ruth Thompson bore much more fruit than in their lives.

God does not require that all of us literally die in order to bear much fruit. But we cannot bear abundant fruit without reckoning—counting—ourselves dead to sin, to self and to anything else that may hinder our fruit bearing. Over and over in my ministry I have had to experience death before fruitfulness.

I "died" to a "daughter" church

After Donna and I had been in Omaha several years, we felt it was time for Christ Community Church to begin a "daughter" church across the river in Council Bluffs, Iowa.

With some 10 Council Bluffs families who had been attending Christ Community Church, we started a home Bible study. It was our expectation that the Bible study, in time, would develop into a full-blown church.

At first the Bible study grew a little. But then to our dismay we began losing one family after another. One moved to Texas, another to Florida, still another to California. Six months after our start, our nucleus was down to three families. And then our lead couple, Al and Brenda Biere, announced they had decided to move back home to Des Moines. What a discouraging situation!

Driving home that Wednesday night, I said glumly to Donna, "Honey, tonight I die to this daughter church. Right now I am burying the whole idea! If God wants a church in Council Bluffs, He will have to resurrect it and build it His way and in His time. I'm finished!"

Something amazing happened. I returned the next Wednesday evening prepared to officiate at the "funeral." But to my great surprise Al and Brenda told us they had changed their minds about moving. Instead, they had decided to commit themselves wholeheartedly to establishing a new church in Council Bluffs.

The Bible study began to grow. New couples joined the group almost every week. To make room, we moved the study to a fire station hall. When we outgrew that, we rented an old church building that had been used for a catering business. The group called a full-time pastor. Then they purchased 10 acres of strategic land and erected a building with a sanctuary seating 300.

Today there is a thriving new congregation in Council Bluffs—Sherwood Community Church. God worked a marvelous miracle that has brought great glory to His Name. When I "died" to *my* plans and *my* efforts, God was able to work.

Samuel Rutherford, 17th-century Scottish theologian, said, "God is no idle Husbandman; He purposeth a crop." By that he meant that God, like a faithful farmer, will do what is necessary to make us fruit-bearers. When our lives yield abundantly, God is glorified.

2. His Power

Our ability as branches to bear fruit does not rest in ourselves. Its source is Christ, the Vine. He said,

> If you remain in me and my words remain in you, ask whatever you wish, and it will be given you. (15:7)

"But," I hear you questioning, "how in practical terms do I tap into Christ's enabling power?"

To such a question Christ might ask in response, "What is your objective? Is it fruit-bearing? Trust in Me, obey Me, ask Me in prayer. By My Spirit, like sap flowing from vine trunk to branches, I will grant you the power to bear abundant fruit."

In Chapters 3 and 4 we looked in detail at the essential role of the Holy Spirit in empowering us for witness and fruit bearing. I shall not, therefore, in this chapter spend time on what we have covered earlier. The Holy Spirit is the Spirit of Jesus ministering in our lives as we yield fully to God in obedience. It is His power that enables us to "bear abundant fruit."

How often Christ's power is made perfect in the weakest branches! I think back to a 72-year-old retired Vietnamese pastor, Phan dinh Lieu. Both his strength and memory were failing. But in his advanced years he still bore much fruit. Hence I invited him to spend a month evangelizing with me so that I could learn the secret of his fruitfulness.

Together we ministered in three villages where the gospel had never been preached. In each, we slept on cots in a little tent. During the daylight hours I went from house to house witnessing to the people about Jesus. Because of my associate's feebleness, he stayed in the tent and prayed. Whenever I returned to the tent I found him sitting on the edge of the cot with a towel over his head to keep out the distractions while he prayed. Each evening as the temperature dropped, his strength increased, and he preached with unusual power. As the month of ministry came to an end, I counted 100 conversions and three new churches! It was a lesson I shall never forget. Our true source of power for fruitfulness is in the Vine.

3. His Purpose

Jesus suggests another factor in His remarks about fruitfulness. God has a purpose in our bearing much fruit.

Someone has aptly stated that the two most important days in people's lives are the day they were born and the day they discover *why* they were born.

Early in my Christian experience, while attending Hampden DuBose Academy, a Christian high school founded by a Presbyterian minister, I learned the Westminster Shorter Catechism. The very first point in that catechism still remains indelibly in my memory, probably because it answered clearly and biblically the question of why I was born:

Q. What is man's chief end?

A. Man's chief end is to glorify God and to enjoy Him forever.

How can a person best glorify God? In His remarks to His disciples Jesus answers that question:

> This is to my Father's glory, that you bear
> much fruit, showing yourselves to be my
> disciples. (15:8)

Later, Jesus states unequivocally the supreme
purpose for which He chose each of us:

> I chose you and appointed you to go and
> bear fruit—fruit that will last. (15:16)

The grape vine produces some of the most
sought-after fruit known to mankind. In contrast to much of the other fruit-bearing flora,
the grape vine expends all its strength on its
fruit. The trunk and branches of the grape vine
must be supported by trellis or arbor. The
grape vine's wood is valueless for construction
or furniture. No one uses grape vines to
beautify a park. Grape wood, however dry,
will not burn well in a fireplace. Only the fruit
has value. Grapes are the sole purpose of the
grape vine.

Likewise we Christians are in this world for
one overriding purpose. We have been saved
not simply to escape sin's power or the fires of
hell. God has delivered us not that we may
enjoy a happy, prosperous life here on earth.
He chose us and saved us to bear fruit!

But having said that, we need to clarify in our
thinking two important matters: what Jesus
meant by "fruit" and the degree of fruitfulness
He seeks from us.

A definition of fruitfulness

Usually we define our terms at the beginning. I have waited until now because that seems to be what Jesus did when He spoke to His disciples. In His discourse He has mentioned fruit and fruitfulness a number of times (15:2, 4, 5, 8). Evidently Jesus assumed His disciples knew what He meant by *fruit*. Well, what did He mean?

I suggest that He referred to two kinds of fruit: the "fruit of the Spirit" (Galatians 5:22–23) and the fruit of personal witness—fruit that He appointed them to "go and bear" (15:16). The first is evident in our lives; the latter depends on our lips. Consider with me first the fruit of the Spirit.

Jesus does not describe all the fruit listed in Galatians 5:22–23: love, joy, peace, patience, kindness, goodness, faithfulness, gentleness and self-control. Rather, He alludes to the first two as though they were suggestive of all the others. Notice how Jesus refers to love:

> As the Father has loved me, so have I loved you. Now remain in my love. If you obey my commands, you will remain in my love, just as I have obeyed my Father's commands and remain in his love. . . . My command is this: Love each other as I have loved you. Greater love has no one than this, that he lay down his life for his

friends. . . . This is my command: Love each other. (15:9–17)

Nine times Jesus uses the word *love*. In each case it is the word for divine, sacrificial love. Jesus is not speaking of sentimental love or natural affection, but rather of the "agape" love that moved Him to lay down His life at Calvary.

Notice also the sequence, which is significant. First Jesus refers to His love, then to our love. He says if we remain in Him we can draw upon His divine love to love one another. There are people whom you and I cannot love apart from Jesus' help and His own love flowing through us. That is why agape love is called the fruit of the Spirit. God gives it only as we remain in Christ the Vine.

Not simply love, but joy

Jesus also refers to another fruit of the Spirit:

I have told you this so that my joy may be in you and that your joy may be complete. (15:11)

Again, the sequence is the same. First, Jesus' joy and then His joy in us. And the joy He gives is full and complete! Christ's true disciples, if they are filled with the Spirit, will be full of His joy in every circumstance. If you see people who call themselves Christians but are perpetually gloomy and morose, they are living contradictions. Christians who abide in the "Vine" will through the fullness of the Holy Spirit "speak to one another with psalms, hymns and spiritual songs." They will "sing and make music in [their] heart[s] to the Lord, always giving thanks to God the Father for everything, in the name of [their] Lord Jesus Christ" (Ephesians 5:19–20).

Some interpreters of John 15 believe the fruit of the Spirit is the *only* fruit Jesus refers to. But careful investigation of the text reveals another kind of fruit. First, Christ tells His disciples that they will bear this fruit by *going*:

> You did not choose me, but I chose you and appointed you to go and bear fruit. (15:16)

The statement seems to be in anticipation of Jesus' Great Commission that several weeks later He would give His disciples. Second, He tells them that the fruit will exhibit stability or permanence:

> . . . fruit that will last. (15:16)

The words point not simply to decision-making but to disciple-making—another focus of Christ's last command. Third, as Jesus continues His remarks to the disciples, He comes right out and speaks clearly of witnessing:

> When the Counselor comes, whom I will send to you from the Father, the Spirit of truth who goes out from the Father, he will testify about me. And you also must testify, for you have been with me from the beginning. (15:26–27)

Again, the same sequence is evident. First, the Spirit witnesses to the disciples about Christ. Then the disciples are to witness to others.

Is it not a glorious thought? God chose you, saved you and left you in the world for the noble purpose of bearing fruit—both the fruit of godly living and the fruit of faithful witness. And both are made possible through the power of His Holy Spirit.

The degrees of fruitfulness

Having defined *fruit*, we now notice the *degrees of fruitfulness*. Jesus speaks about our *bearing fruit* (15:2) and implies God's desire that we bear even *more fruit* (also 15:2). Then Jesus says that by remaining in Him we shall bear *much fruit* (15:5). Finally, He adds the dimension of permanence: *fruit that will last* (15:16). All this suggests to us that God desires not only that we bear fruit, but that as we grow in our Christian life our fruitfulness will increase.

One of the godliest men I ever knew was Keil D. Garrison, my favorite professor at Nyack

(NY) College. Some friends who knew him when he was a young missionary in India said that back then he exhibited much stubbornness, impatience and an unruly temper. But as he aged, he evidenced more and more of the fruit of the Spirit. When I knew him, I found it difficult to believe that he could ever have been anything but a loving, humble, peaceable saint. It was a lesson I shall long remember in the possibilities for each of us to increase in spiritual fruitfulness.

God also purposes that we exhibit increasing fruitfulness in our witness. And happily this is possible if we will tap into His power and follow His biblical model.

I must confess that for the first 19 years of my life, I bore no fruit through witnessing—not even after Jesus Christ saved me from my sins. Although I testified often of Christ, I never saw anyone come to Him for salvation. Knowing I would one day be serving God overseas, I began to pray that He would give me fruit here in America.

The summer after my first year of college, I traveled 8,000 miles with a male quartet from the school. One night in Erie, Pennsylvania, after singing in the town park, I had the joy of sharing the gospel with a young man about my age. When he invited Christ into his life, I nearly exploded with excitement.

Four years later, when Donna and I were appointed to serve as missionaries in Vietnam, I prayed that God would enable us to bear much fruit among the people of that land. God answered prayer, and to our great joy we saw a continual increase of people coming to Christ. It was our privilege to witness in villages, prisons, military hospitals, refugee camps and youth centers. We saw many people added to the Evangelical Church of Vietnam. But I was not satisfied with the measure of fruitfulness I saw those 20 years in Vietnam.

God desires multiplication

You see, God in His first command to mankind did not say, "Be fruitful and *add*." He said, "Be fruitful and increase in number; fill the earth" (Genesis 1:28). That implies *multiplication*!

Someone said it is better to plant apple trees than merely to pick apples. Or, to be consistent with the metaphor we have been looking at in this chapter, it is better to plant grape vines than merely to pick grapes!

"What does that have to do with witnesses?" you ask. Simply this: It is far better to train people to be effective witnesses than it is merely to witness. Then by multiplying the number of persons witnessing you will multiply the number of people turning to Christ Jesus.

Jesus spent some of His time evangelizing. But most of His time and energies were concentrated on training His disciples—who, in turn, would be His witnesses. That was the secret of the church's multiplication. Yes, Jesus picked some fruit. But more important, He planted fruit-bearing "trees."

I have already related how in Hong Kong, after the fall of South Vietnam, God led me to the witnessing strategy called Evangelism Explosion. That word *explosion* refers to the multiplication of witnesses through on-the-job training. Better yet, it means equipping *trainers* who will teach others how to witness effectively. I cannot express in words the thrill of seeing through "E.E." my evangelism/discipleship ministry multiply many, many times over.

In our final year in Hong Kong, I had the joy of leading to Christ a Chinese optometrist, Edmund. That was "fruit picking." But then Edmund enlisted in our E.E. training and himself became an effective witness for Christ. A few months after our family settled in Omaha, I received a phone call from Edmund. He was in Los Angeles, on his way to Florida.

"Pastor Tom," he said, "since you left Hong Kong I have led 26 people to Christ. But now I want to do as you did and train others to become witnesses. So I'm on my way to Fort Lauderdale to be qualified as a teacher-trainer."

What a delight it was to know that Edmund was on his way to being a fruit-bearing tree in Hong Kong, carrying on the work Donna and I had begun!

Where do you stand?

As you have meditated on the theme of John 15, how do you see yourself? Of the four kinds of branches referred to, which are you? Are you one who bears *no* fruit? Do you bear *some* fruit? Do you bear *more* fruit? Are you one who bears *much* fruit?

If you are bearing no fruit, could it be because you have no relation to Christ? Perhaps you have never, through simple faith, trusted Him as your Savior. If you think that is your problem, let me again refer you to page 330 of this book.

Or perhaps your life manifests mostly leaves. You need the *pruning* shears of the heavenly Gardener to clear away those hindrances in your life to fruit-bearing.

Could it be you just have not known how to tap into God's *power*—the power the Holy Spirit alone can give you? You have tried to be a disciple in your own strength, and the results have been disappointing.

Maybe you have never realized that God's *purpose* for you as a branch is to bear fruit—abundant, abiding fruit. You have never been trained to win people to Christ, equipped for a ministry of evangelism to relatives, friends and acquaintances or equipped so that you can train others to become fruitful soul-winners.

On the basis of what Jesus said to His disciples, I can declare that God wants every

Christian to reproduce Christ's character—the fruit of love, joy, peace, patience, kindness, goodness, faithfulness, self-control. He will do it through you if you will let Him.

Jesus also wants you to obey His Great Commission to go and bear fruit through witnessing. This, too, must be through the power of His Spirit.

I want to bear *abundant* fruit. Do you?

If so, stay tuned as we discuss being life-style witnesses in Chapter 6.

Study Questions

John 15

1. Which of the following do you most resemble and why: cactus, tumbleweed, oak tree, grape vine, weeping willow?
2. What do you understand to be the fruit about which Jesus was speaking in John 15?
3. In light of this chapter, how would you describe a "disciple"?
4. Think back over your life to your most fruitful year. How and why was it fruitful?
5. What "pruning" experiences has God brought into your life and what were the results?
6. If eternal life never ends, how do you explain verse 6—branches being cast into the fire?
7. In light of this chapter, what is a Christian's purpose on earth?

8. What does the statement, "It's better to plant apple trees than to merely pick apples" mean to you and how are you reflecting this principle in your life?

CHAPTER 6

Becoming Life-Style Witnesses

John 1

THE MOST ABUNDANT, abiding fruit (the subject of our last chapter) comes to the person who makes witnessing a way of life in the context of personal relationships. That holds true for church congregations, too—including yours.

Church growth experts did a survey of 15,000 church-going Christians, asking them who the principle witness was who brought them to Christ. Interestingly, 75–90 percent (depending on the church) of those interviewed responded that they had been influenced through family, friends, associates—someone with whom they had a personal relationship.

But this is not just a 20th-century phenomenon. It was the principal way the gospel spread in New Testament times. A good illustration of it occurs in John 1. Although John 1 might be outlined in a number of ways, for our study of life-style witnessing, I shall divide it into three parts: *the Word* (the message), *the witness* (the messenger) and *the world* of the messenger (his or her mission field)—the people in his or her network of relationships.

1. The Word

First, the Word. A witness must have a message, and John tells us that in gospel witness our message is the Word—Jesus Christ. John informs us of two important truths about Christ: *who He is* and *why He came*.

As to His identity, Jesus is the infinite God-Man.

> In the beginning was the Word, and the Word was with God, and the Word was God. He was with God in the beginning.
> Through him all things were made; without him nothing was made that has been made. In him was life, and that life was the light of men. (John 1:1–4)

This Word, Jesus Christ, is not just a national president, like George Washington was, or the chairman of an earthly power, like Mao Tse-tung was. He is Co-Creator with God the Father of all matter from galaxies to sub-atomic particles. He is the Sustainer of all things, most importantly of life itself.

John moves from Jesus' deity to His humanity. He tells us that this Word who was with God the Father from eternity past became a human being and lived on this earth among human beings.

> The Word became flesh and made His dwelling among us. (1:14)

Being God, He could identify with God's plans and fulfill God's ministry and mission on earth. Being Man, He could identify with us and our needs.

John also tells us why Jesus came. He came, first, to reveal an invisible God to mankind.

> No one has ever seen God, but God the One and Only, who is at the Father's side, has made him known. (1:18)

Jesus came to reveal God to us

It is a beautiful metaphor. God the Word—Jesus Christ—came to let us know what God the Father is like. A word is a written or spoken vehicle used to express one's invisible thoughts and feelings. "A penny for your thoughts!" we say to someone. In effect we are asking the other person to put in words what we cannot otherwise guess. That is the purpose of words and sentences. They convey ideas, feelings, meaning. Christ the God-Man came from the Father to reveal to us the invisible Father God, to express His love and to convey His will.

But John offers another reason why the Word, Jesus Christ, came. Having revealed God to mankind, He became Himself the sacrificial Lamb to redeem mankind to God.

> . . . John [the Baptist] saw Jesus coming toward him and said, "Look, the Lamb of God, who takes away the sin of the world!" (1:29)

Every Jew knew the purpose of a lamb. A lamb was slaughtered and its blood shed as a sacrifice for sin. The lamb died in place of the sinner so the sinner could live forgiven and redeemed. Jesus, the Lamb of God, came to do all that for mankind, not only in that age but also in every age and for all time. He came to redeem us.

That is who this Word, Christ Jesus, is and why He came. He is the infinite God-Man. He came to *reveal* God to us and to *redeem* us from our sins.

What an important message! What a wonderful Word we have in Jesus Christ to share with others!

2. The Witness

The second aspect of life-style witnessing John introduces to us is the *witness* himself.

> There came a man who was sent from God; his name was John. (1:6)

We know him as John the Baptist. Twice the Apostle John who wrote this gospel calls John the Baptist a "witness":

> He came as a witness to testify . . .
> He came only as a witness . . . (1:7–8)

The Apostle John has a unique writing style. He is not as orderly and logical as Paul. Sometimes it is difficult to follow his thoughts, as in this first chapter where he alternates between Jesus and John the Baptist:

> Jesus the Word (1:1–5)
> John the witness (1:6–8)
> Jesus the Light (1:9–14)
> John the witness—again (1:15ff.)

But that is not an accident! There is a reason for this arrangement of the text. God sent *both* Jesus and John, the Word and the witness. Their ministries were interdependent. This can best be illustrated by referring to the two chief metaphors of the chapter. As we have already seen, Jesus is called the *Word*. And in 1:23 John the Baptist refers to himself as a *voice*.

A voice is an audible sound, an utterance made through the mouth to convey by word or groups of words what we call a message. The interdependence of words and voice we illustrate when we worship in song. First, we read words in our hymnal. Then we use our voices to convey those words in song. Just so, John the Baptist needed Jesus, and Jesus needed John. As wonderful as Jesus' ministries of revelation and redemption were, they would be of marginal benefit without the witness of John the Baptist.

It is the same today. Jesus needs people sent by God to be witnesses. He needs me. He needs you. I suggest, therefore, that you personalize verse 6. "There came a man (woman) who was sent from God; his (her) name was . . ."—and then write your name in place of "John."

Next, I want you to see something else very important about a witness.

> [John the Baptist] came as a witness to testify concerning that light, so that through him all men might believe. (1:7)

A witness wants people to believe his or her message. A witness is concerned about his or her credibility.

The Chinese have a very interesting character

for the word *believe*. Their characters, as you know, are picture symbols of the words they convey. Their character for *believe* is composed of two picture symbols. The one on the right is the character for *word*. The one on the left is the character for *man*. In their symbolism, they are saying that belief is dependent upon the integrity of the speaker and that the integrity of a speaker is only possible when that person's life and lips give forth the same message!

Just so, John goes on to describe the *life* of the believable witness. He enumerates four traits essential to the witness.

A *witness must be born—a second time*

First, he or she must *be born*—actually, be born again.

> To all who received [Jesus, the true Light], to those who believed in his name, he gave the right to become children of God— children born not of natural descent, nor of human decision or a husband's will, but born of God. (1:12–13)

When Christ came into the world not everyone trusted Him for salvation. But those who did were born into God's family and became God's children. Unfortunately, there is a false teaching in the world today endorsed by many liberal churches. It goes by the name of universalism and often uses such phrases as "the fatherhood of God" and "the brotherhood of man"—meaning that by virtue of creation we are all one family and children of God.

Very clearly the Bible distinguishes between physical and spiritual birth. Physical birth involves "human decision or a husband's will." The resulting baby is a three-dimensional, flesh-and-blood physical being. Spiritual birth, as the term implies, has to do with God's Spirit bringing life to the inner "us," until then "dead in [our] transgression and sins" (Ephesians 2:1). Spiritual birth will have its effect upon our three-dimensional, flesh-and-blood lives, but the two are not the same.

Later John reports about Nicodemus, "a member of the Jewish ruling council," who "came to Jesus at night" (John 3:1–2). Nicodemus was religious. He was, in fact, a Pharisee—of all Jews the most strict in their religious observances. He had political power. He was wealthy, later donating expensive spices for Jesus' burial. He was cultured; he addressed Jesus as "Rabbi."

But all that impressive pedigree still left Nicodemus short. "Jesus declared, 'I tell you the truth, no one can see the kingdom of God unless he is born again' " (3:3).

If you are to be a witness to Jesus Christ, you must be born spiritually into God's family. If a person blind from birth cannot describe the beauties of a sunset, if a bachelor cannot communicate the joys of a happy marriage, neither can someone who has never experienced God's new birth be a witness for Jesus Christ.

A witness must behold

A witness not only needs to be born, but, second, he or she needs to *behold*. The dictionary defines a witness as one who has personal knowledge of a thing. Witnesses are important in our courts of law. "I saw it happen" and "I was there" are powerful words to juries. Notice the use of *saw*, *see* and *have seen* as John the Baptist makes reference to his firsthand knowledge of Jesus:

> Then John gave this testimony: "I saw the Spirit come down from heaven as a dove and remain on Him. . . .The one who sent me to baptize with water told me, 'The man on whom you see the Spirit come down and remain is he who will baptize with the Holy Spirit.' I have seen and I testify that this is the Son of God." (1:32–34)

Of course, first-century witnesses such as John the Baptist, living in Palestine, had opportunity to see Jesus. But what about us who live 2,000 years later? How can we behold Jesus Christ?

The Apostle Paul tells us that when we turn to the Lord Jesus, the "veil" that formerly hid

Him from view is "taken away" (2 Corinthians 3:16). "And we," Paul goes on to say, "who with unveiled faces all reflect the Lord's glory, are being transformed into his likeness with ever-increasing glory, which comes from the Lord, who is the Spirit" (3:18).

How, in practical terms, do we "behold" the Lord Jesus? John declared that Jesus is the Word of God. God has revealed that living Word—Jesus—in His written Word, the Bible. We must spend quality time in the Bible. God also invites us to come into His presence in worship:

> Come, let us bow down in worship,
>   let us kneel before the LORD our Maker;
> for he is our God
>   and we are the people of his pasture,
>   the flock under his care. (Psalm 95:6–7)

As we behold Christ Jesus, "the image of the invisible God" (Colossians 1:15), in the Word, in worship and in prayer, the glory of Christ in our lives will make our witness much more powerful.

The effect of the glory of Christ in a person's life was demonstrated to me during an evangelistic meeting in Vietnam. At the conclusion of my sermon a man came forward to receive Christ as his Savior. Afterward, I inquired what had especially prompted him to respond. I expected him to mention something I had said in my message. Instead, he pointed to a back corner of the church.

"Do you see that man back there?" the new convert asked. "He's a deacon in your church. I've been watching him for some time. And I decided I wanted whatever it was he has."

That Vietnamese deacon had been beholding the glory of Christ and his daily life reflected that glory.

A witness must be full

There is still a third imperative. We must *be full*.

> From the fullness of his grace we have all received one blessing after another. (John 1:16)

Grace is a rich word! It means "God's riches at Christ's expense"—as someone has put it. Grace is God's unmerited favor. It is God's free forgiveness of our sins because Christ paid our death penalty when He died on the cross. It is eternal life that we receive at the point of our salvation. But it is much more. It is "one blessing after another," as John puts it.

Grace is multifaceted. It is the beauty and graciousness we receive from God's indwelling Spirit. It is the divine enabling—power, authority—granted by the Holy Spirit to be an effective witness for Christ. It is what Jesus referred to when He promised, "You will receive power when the Holy Spirit comes on you; and you will be my witnesses" (Acts 1:8). It is what those first believers experienced at Pentecost when "all of them were filled with the Holy Spirit and began to speak in other tongues" (Acts 2:4). Their miraculous ability to witness in the languages of the people who had converged on Jerusalem from all parts of the Roman Empire led to the conversion of 3,000.

Twice the Apostle John speaks of grace and truth in relation to Jesus Christ:

> The Word became flesh and made his dwelling among us. We have seen his glory, the glory of the One and Only, who came from the Father, full of grace and truth. (1:14)

> The law was given through Moses; grace and truth came through Jesus Christ. (1:17)

I cannot help but think that the sequence—first grace, then truth—is significant. It is possible for us to be full of truth: gospel outlines, Scripture verses, illustrations, logic, Greek, Hebrew, sound theology, impeccable apologetics. But having all that great storehouse of truth, our witness will still be ineffective if we lack God's grace in our lives. The wealth of truth in our heads must be accompanied by an abundance of grace in our hearts.

They tell of a male professor who prepared an eloquent lecture on the subject of falling in love. There was one problem: he was a bachelor who had never been in love. As the story goes, he took his manuscript to a female secretary to type. When his eyes met hers, something powerful happened! Suddenly he was experiencing what he had struggled to write about from theory.

So with Christianity. It is "better caught than taught." When people see the grace of God and the beauty of Christ in your life, they are attracted to Him and impacted by your witness in a most powerful way.

A vivid illustration of this was the witness of John the Baptist. Matthew has given us our most detailed account of that ministry. If John the Baptist were living today, he would fail every seminary course on evangelistic preaching or personal evangelism.

Seminaries advise us to fish where the fish are—to preach in places where we can gather a large crowd. But John preached in the "Desert of Judea" (Matthew 3:1), a place obviously lacking people.

Seminaries advise us that dress is important. We should give careful attention to our attire. But John wore "clothes . . . made of camel's hair" (3:4)—a cheap, coarse cloth.

Seminaries might advise us to pay attention to diet: the proper kinds of food and the right amounts, so that we can be at our physical best as we minister. John's diet was an unbelievable mixture of "locusts and wild honey" (3:4).

Seminaries stress the importance of an introduction that compliments the audience, puts them on the evangelist's side, wins a hearing for the rest of the message. John begins his message by calling the Pharisees and Sadducees in his audience a "brood of vipers" (3:7).

Despite such apparent blunders, John attracted crowds "from Jerusalem and all Judea and the whole region of the Jordan" (3:5). They came not simply to listen, but "confessing their sins, they were baptized by him in the Jordan River" (3:6).

How do you explain this amazing response to a witness who seemed to be doing everything wrong? Could it be that he was full of grace and truth? What a message for us who want to be fruitful witnesses to our generation!

A witness must be vocal

But there is a fourth factor essential to effective witness. We must also *be vocal*. There are Christians who in practice absolve themselves from sharing the gospel by rationalizing, "I witness by my life. What counts is my walk." It sounds commendable, but it just is not biblical.

Jesus Christ commands us to "preach (announce) the good news to all creation" (Mark 16:15). As we saw earlier, all of the believers, scattered from Jerusalem by persecution, "preached the word wherever they went" (Acts 8:1, 4). Paul asks, "How can they believe in the one of whom they have not heard? And how can they hear without someone preaching to them?" (Romans 10:14).

John the Baptist, as we noted, over and over vocalized his witness. Listen to him cry out to those who had come to see and hear him:

> The next day John saw Jesus coming toward him and said, "Look, the Lamb of God, who takes away the sin of the world!" (1:29)

> When [John the Baptist] saw Jesus passing by, he said, "Look, the Lamb of God!" (1:36)

It has been aptly observed that when people witness only with their *lives*, they witness only to themselves. But when they witness with their *lips*, they witness to Jesus Christ. That certainly does not mean that you must give a lawyer's defense to the gospel. You are sent by God as an envoy to witness. By that I mean you are to give a firsthand, personal account of your conversion to Christ. The blind man healed by Jesus had a brief but very powerful testimony. He said: "One thing I do know. I was blind but now I see!" (John 9:25).

George Cutting, author of *Safety, Certainty and*

Enjoyment, tells of bicycling down a street in an English village. As he passed a certain cottage he felt impelled by the Holy Spirit to call out— in John the Baptist's words—"Look, the Lamb of God, who takes away the sin of the world!" Then he repeated it.

Six months later Cutting was evangelizing that area, visiting from house to house. He came to the house where he had been impressed to vocally witness on his previous trip. When a woman came to the door, he asked her if she was saved.

"Oh, yes," the woman replied joyfully. "Six months ago I was in great distress about the salvation of my soul. I pleaded for God's help. Then a voice cried, 'Look, the Lamb of God, who takes away the sin of the world!' I asked God to repeat what He had said, and the voice repeated the same message!" George Cutting had been that brief but powerful vocal witness.

To summarize, if you wish to be an effective witness to the Word (Jesus), you must, like the first century envoys, *be born, behold, be full* and *be vocal.*

3. The World

Jesus came as God's eternal *Word.* He died for our sins and rose from the dead. He spells out reconciliation for all who put their trust in Him. But the Word can only be known as vocal *witnesses* speak of Him. And where can these witnesses best expect a hearing? In their *world* of friends, relatives and acquaintances—the people most apt to believe their testimony.

What do I mean by *world*? I mean that pattern of relationships that we find in every society on earth. We might call it the network of people who touch us and whom we touch in our normal circumstances. Some of these relationships are closer than others, but all afford us choice opportunity for witness. It is through this network of relationships that the gospel travels best, as the church survey earlier cited affirms.

But this in not just a 20th-century phenomenon. It was the primary way the gospel spread in New Testament times. We want to notice in John 1 how the gospel followed such a network.

Relatives

Jesus and John the Baptist were probably cousins. Jesus' mother, Mary, and John's mother, Elizabeth, were blood related, although we do not know precisely the relationship. When Jesus "came to that which was his own" (John 1:11), the large majority of His own people did not receive Him. But some did receive Him, for the Apostle John goes on to say,

> Yet to all who received him, to those who believed in his name, he gave the right to become children of God—children born

not of natural descent . . . but . . . of God. (1:12–13)

John the Baptist certainly was one of those who believed, for he testifies to his faith in Jesus:

> The next day John saw Jesus coming toward him and said, "Look, the Lamb of God, who takes away the sin of the world! (1:29)

> . . . I have seen and I testify that this is the Son of God. (1:34)

Evidently Jesus had witnessed to His earthly cousin and brought him to saving faith.

There are many examples of Christians leading their relatives to Christ. I think of John whose wife Becky found that her 80-year-old uncle was suffering from terminal cancer. This elderly man had been like a stepdad to Becky. Although a church-goer, he was not ready for heaven. John, who had cultivated a loving relationship with Becky's uncle and who had been trained how to witness, reviewed his gospel presentation, then visited him in the hospital. There he led the elderly man to faith in Christ.

Associates

John the Baptist had some associates—disciples—to whom he witnessed. We are told that they also trusted in Jesus Christ.

> The next day John was there again with two of his disciples. When he saw Jesus passing by, he said, "Look, the Lamb of God!"
> When the two disciples heard him say this, they followed Jesus. (1:35–37)

Wayne, a member of our Omaha congregation, often witnessed to his work associates. One day he shared Christ with a fellow welder, Kevin. Kevin at first rebuffed Wayne. But he could not get from his mind several of the things Wayne had said. A few months later Kevin went to Wayne and inquired more about the gospel. And gave his heart to Jesus Christ.

Days later Kevin was killed in an accident involving his pickup truck. Wayne attended the funeral of his welder friend. A few weeks later he was able to lead Kevin's mother to faith in Christ. How glad Wayne was that he had been equipped and faithful to witness to his work associate!

Family

Reading on in John 1, we come to another part of a typical messenger's world. One of John the Baptist's associates had a family member whom he brought to Jesus.

Andrew, Simon Peter's brother, was one of the two who heard what John had said and who had followed Jesus. The first thing Andrew did was to find his brother Simon and tell him, "We have found the Messiah" (that is, the Christ). And he brought him to Jesus. (1:40–42)

Over and over in New Testament times we find Christians winning their family members to Christ.

When Paul and Silas testified to the Philippian jailer, Paul said, "Believe in the Lord Jesus, and you will be saved—you and your household" (Acts 16:31).

Two young women in our congregation spent Thanksgiving with their grandmother. As they were sitting around the table, their grandmother asked, "What have you girls been doing in Omaha that's new?"

"E.E.," one of the two replied.

"And what is 'E.E.'?"

"We're learning to ask people some very interesting questions."

Their grandmother wanted to know what the questions were. To their surprise, the two young women discovered that their grandmother was trusting in good works to qualify her for heaven.

Before the two women returned to Omaha, they had been able to lead their grandmother to faith in Christ.

Friends

There is one last reference in John 1 to a messenger's world. It is a reference to friends. There is no indication that Nathanael was related to Philip or that the two were work associates. But it does seem apparent that they were friends. And Philip, like a true friend, did the best thing anyone could do for a friend. He brought him to Jesus.

> The next day Jesus decided to leave for Galilee. Finding Philip, he said to him, "Follow me."
> Philip, like Andrew and Peter, was from the town of Bethsaida. Philip found Nathanael and told him, "We have found the one Moses wrote about in the Law, and about whom the prophets also wrote—Jesus of Nazareth, the son of Joseph." (1:43–45)

It is not difficult to cite examples of people from our congregation who have led friends to Christ. For example, Denise exercised regularly with her neighbor. One day as the two were walking, Denise's neighbor told Denise that she saw something different about her. She wondered if Denise could explain what the difference was. The two friends sat on the curb while Denise, well-trained to share her faith, led the other woman to Christ.

Why so fruitful?

Why is witnessing to your world of family, other relatives, neighbors, work associates so abundantly fruitful? First, because you are witnessing to them as a person they trust rather than as a stranger. Second, you are able to give them an unhurried witness, repeated if necessary over a period of weeks, months and even years. Third, you have opportunity to demonstrate to them by your life-style the power of the gospel you are sharing. Fourth, you have a trusted relationship that, once they believe, makes follow-up much more natural and effective. Fifth, if they do not already have a church home, they will probably want to attend and become a part of your church.

At Christ Community Church we have developed a new evangelistic thrust in our outreach ministry, and we're calling it *OIKOS OUTREACH*. What does *OIKOS* mean? As our senior pastor quipped, you would think it is . . .

- A baby oyster
- An Australian bird
- An aboriginal fetish
- The uppermost portion of a circus tent
- The central gear in a planetary gear set

Actually, it's none of the above. *OIKOS* in the New Testament is translated "household." The term occurs several times in the book of Acts in conjunction with salvation. It seems when the head of a household got saved, his household got saved. And the household sometimes included more than immediate family members. In Cornelius' case it included servants, soldiers, relatives, close friends and others.

With this as a biblical precedent and basis we have developed this *OIKOS OUTREACH* ministry as the primary evangelistic strategy for our church. You would think that the short hand version for it would be OO, but it's actually "*OO4*."

What does the "4" stand for? It stands for a number of things. Primarily it stands for four categories of people we are trying to reach: friends, relatives, associates and neighbors.

The "4" also stands for four times a year we train our people in Sunday School how to reach out to their "oikos" with a loving witness. Four times a year we also have a Friendship Sunday specially geared for visitors. This is usually two weeks after the training in the Sunday School class.

Recently, Louise in my Sunday School class came up to me all bubbly and said, "Pastor, I can't wait to tell you what I'm doing in my local community! I've started evangelizing all of my neighbors. One of them asked me where I got my enthusiasm for this, and I told her it was from my Sunday School teacher, and I haven't even had E.E. yet!"

This was after four lessons on *OO4*, and now

she has a Bible study in Romans going for her neighbors.

We have developed materials for teaching and leading this new thrust. Christian Publications has now begun publishing the materials, so that other churches can adapt the materials to their situations. You may want to look into this for your church.

Do you realize that you may be the only true Christian your family, friends, neighbors and associates know? They may never meet another person who can introduce them to Jesus Christ. They are your responsibility. They are the world into which Jesus Christ sends you as a witness.

Perhaps you are thinking, "Me? *Me* win my family and friends to Christ? Impossible! How could I ever win *anyone*, much less my family, neighbors and associates?"

I have good news for you! With God's help you can win them. And if you will read the next chapter, I will tell you how!

Study Questions

John 1

1. What is the significance of John's calling Jesus "the Word"? What does John tell us about His nature?
2. What is the significance of John the Baptist calling himself a "voice" in verse 23?

3. What biblical traits do you feel should mark the life of a soul-winner in our day?

4. What if Jesus told you today that you are His personal representative in your neighborhood, place of employment, club, school, home? How would you respond? What would you do?

5. Of all of your unsaved friends, relatives, work/school associates or neighbors, who would you say is the most "open" to the gospel? What are some of the things you might do to show him or her love and begin reaching out to him or her?

6. If the way opened for you to share the gospel with that person, what do you think you would do and say?

CHAPTER 7

Winning Lasting Trophies

1 Corinthians 9

EVERYONE WANTS TO BE A WINNER. From earliest childhood people have the desire to come out on top. When my two sons, Jeff and John, were barely able to walk, I discovered a painless way to get them to finish their oatmeal.

"Let's see who can finish first!" I would say. And in a matter of seconds, both boys would polish off the detestable stuff, one of them shouting, "I won!"

Donna and I drove to Minneapolis with an Indian missionary family from our church. As we crossed the border between Iowa and Minnesota, we read a sign announcing that we had come to "the land of 10,000 lakes."

"Well," I said to my fellow passengers, "let's

see who can count the most lakes between here and Minneapolis." Several times I found myself wandering off the uncrowded highway as I looked in all directions for lakes. To the surprise of all of us, the youngest passenger, Sharon, finished with the highest score, exclaiming gleefully, "I won!"

I heard a story of a 70-year-old Irishman who won $65,000 in the Irish sweepstakes. Because he had heart problems, his family feared the exciting news could be fatal to him. So they called for their pastor, a man skilled in breaking shocking news.

"Sir," said the minister to the elderly gentleman, "if you were ever to win 60 or 70 thousand dollars, I'd be interested to know what you would do with it."

"That's easy," replied the Irishman. "First, I'd give the church half of it, and then the other half I'd give to you, Pastor!" Whereupon the pastor fell over dead!

Anyone can be a winner, it has been said—unless there happens to be a second entry. Some people work hard to win beauty contests, others a political election or an athletic competition. Whatever the field, all of us want to come out on top!

The most important arena of life—where we ought to strive hardest—is that of winning people to Jesus Christ. Solomon, whose wisdom was legendary, said, "He who wins souls is wise" (Proverbs 11:30). In a far-ranging vision given to Daniel, God said, "Those who lead many to righteousness [will shine] like the stars for ever and ever" (Daniel 12:3).

There is no comparison

In my lifetime I have won a few tennis trophies and have tasted victory in a few other sports. But there is nothing to compare with the thrill of winning even one person to Jesus Christ. It has been the consuming passion of my life. It is at the center of our Omaha church's purpose statement: "To make disciples of Jesus Christ by *winning them to faith in Christ* and teaching them to obey the Word of Christ."

God wants every one of His people to win other people to Christ Jesus. Those who do so have gained lasting trophies to present someday to King Jesus. One of the greatest chapters in the Bible on the theme of winning people to Christ is First Corinthians 9. In that marvelous section of his letter, Paul defends his apostleship, sets forth his right to financial support and then explains why he forfeits all rights to such support. He goes on to say he is free from all people, but—and this is the essence of Paul's life—he is still a "slave" to them:

> Though I am free and belong to no man, I make myself a slave to everyone, to *win* as many as possible. (9:19)

In his personal references throughout the chapter, Paul gives us insight into six essential elements in winning fellow beings to Christ Jesus: *people* (of course!), *penetration, proclamation, persuasion, preparation, prizes.* We will examine all six elements to see how they apply to us.

1. People

Paul begins by stating clearly that people are the object of his work. He asks,

> Are you not the result of my work in the Lord? (9:1)

Paul's question is especially interesting in light of Acts 18:1–3. There we learn that Paul, newly arrived in Corinth, met two other newcomers to the city: "a Jew named Aquila . . . with his wife Priscilla." Because all three of them were tentmakers by trade, Paul "stayed and worked with them." Clearly Paul's work at Corinth was tentmaking, but why then, in writing to the Corinthians, does he say that the result of his work was people, not tents?

We gain further insight as we continue in Acts 18. "One night the Lord spoke to Paul in a vision: 'Do not be afraid; keep on speaking, do not be silent. For I am with you, and no one is going to attack and harm you, because I have many people in this city.' So Paul stayed for a year and a half, teaching them the word of God" (18:9–11).

Yes, Paul was a tentmaker, but his real, lasting work was people. It reminds me of a Christian baker's response when someone asked him what his work was. "I win people to Christ," he said, "but I bake bread to pay expenses." I like that! Would that more of us might realize that the most lasting work we can do is not to build buildings or head up organizations or create literature or compose songs but to bring people to Jesus Christ.

Unfortunately, we live in a world becoming more and more depersonalized. With increased automation and computerization, we are getting farther and farther from people. We have automatic tellers at our banks, coin-operated vending machines delivering food and drink, and answering machines to handle our telephone calls. At the Orlando airport I boarded an unmanned rail car whose doors opened and closed automatically. A recorded voice told me where and how to stand. It delivered me to the baggage claim area without my meeting a single person.

But long before the development of such dehumanizing machines, people had low estimates of their fellows. Samuel Johnson remarked, "I hate mankind, for I think of myself as one of the best of them, and I know how bad I am." Mark Twain commented, "Man is a creature made at the end of the week

when God was tired." And Will Rogers
quipped, "God made man a little lower than
the angels, and he's been getting lower and
lower ever since."

God has not given up on us

Recently I saw a cartoon of a man and his dog
watching news on television. The dog was
soliloquizing, "Every day I find it harder and
harder to be man's best friend." Someone
defined horse sense as "the common sense that
keeps horses from betting on people."

Horses may not bet on people, but God does!
God created people. He became a person. He
died to redeem people. He is in the business of
transforming people. He makes His home
within people. People are the crowning
wonder of His creation. Every newborn baby is
God's vote for the worth and future of people.

Marvin Rosenthal, writing in *Israel, My Glory*,
tells about a mother who was asked by a census taker how many children she had. She
responded, "Well, there's Billy and Harry and
Martha and—"

"Never mind the names," the census taker interrupted. "Just give me the number!"

"They haven't got numbers," the mother
replied indignantly. "They've all got names."

Today we all have numbers, from Social
Security to driver's license to bank account—a
series of digits in a supercomputer. But the
God who created the staggering billions of

stars above our heads calls each of them by name. To Him each of us is not a number but a name!

What is your estimate of people? Are they precious eternal beings made in the image of God? Are they bodies, minds and souls for whom Christ died on Calvary's rugged cross? Are they people with a never-ending future— in either heaven or hell?

Did you know there are people only *you* can touch for God? Only you will have the golden opportunity to share the message of life with them. They are neighbors, fellow workers, family members, shop keepers, store clerks, waiters and waitresses, insurance agents, students, teachers, repairmen, carpet cleaners. Only you will be in a strategic position to win them to Christ.

Too often we envision "people who need the Lord" in terms of the Danis of Indonesia, the Black Bobos of Mali, the Aucas of Ecuador. We are blind to the people all around us who equally need the Lord. Can you say to someone in Paul's words, "Are you not the result of my work in the Lord?" Can you believe God will use you to win people who are within your everyday network of relationships?

2. Penetration

The next essential element in winning people to Christ is *penetration*. As Paul approached people with the purpose of winning them to faith in Christ, he discovered they were heterogeneous. By that I mean he was surrounded by unrelated, unlike people. The society of that day had diverse customs and cultures, dissimilar values and interests. People were from contrasting backgrounds. Most of them lived in a totally different world from Paul's.

Paul realized that in order to proclaim the message of life to them effectively, he had to penetrate their world. He had to plunge into their society. He had to adapt to their culture, learn their language, conform to their ways of doing, identify with their joys and hurts.

> Though I am free and belong to no man, I make myself a slave to everyone, to win as many as possible. To the Jews I became like a Jew, to win the Jews. To those under the law I became like one under the law, ... so as to win those under the law. To those not having the law I became like one not having the law, . . . so as to win those not having the law. To the weak I became weak, to win the weak. I have become all things to all men so that by all possible means I might save some. (1 Corinthians 9:19–22)

God the Son left heaven and plunged into our sinful, suffering world to seek, to serve, to save us. Paul realized that if he were to save the people of his generation, he would have to do the same.

We, too, must immerse ourselves

As a missionary in Vietnam I saw the absolute necessity of learning the language and customs of the people, of adapting to their ways of living, thinking and doing. It was the only avenue to communicate effectively to them God's message of love and salvation. I found that thoroughly penetrating the Vietnamese world and culture made a tremendous difference. The people would listen to the gospel for hours, fascinated by the fact that I had not only come to their villages but that I had taken the trouble to learn their language and was now willing to eat their food, sleep on their hardwood beds and be at home in their culture.

Returning later to America, I found the same need for penetration. Donna and I soon learned that to share the gospel with mid-westerners in Omaha, we had to understand the ways of people in the midwest. Very quickly we became "Big Red" fans, supporting University of Nebraska football. We joined a local tennis club. We built various bridges to our neighbors.

Gradually we learned the values of the people we were seeking to reach. More than that, we learned how to communicate the message of heaven in language the Nebraskans understood. Just as in Vietnam and Hong Kong, we had to identify with them in their likes, their needs, their interests. We had to earn the right to share with them the good news.

Lloyd Andrews, of Council Bluffs, Iowa, graphically demonstrated an understanding of penetration as he was on his way home from work one day. Right in front of him he witnessed a single car accident. The car was "totalled," but the driver climbed out unscathed. Lloyd could have driven by, remaining uninvolved. Instead, he decided to plunge into this driver's crisis. Pulling his car off the road, he asked the woman how he could help. She said that after talking to the police and filing an accident report, she would appreciate a ride home. The police investigation and report took an hour. Then Lloyd and his passenger began the 50-mile trip to her home in the countryside.

"You know," the woman said as they were driving, "I could have been killed!" Lloyd had already earned the right to speak, and he knew what to say. Before the trip was over, the woman had given her heart to Jesus Christ.

Not usually is rapport built that fast. Often it takes months—sometimes even years—to build trust and openness to the gospel. It took Donna and me 10 years to reach our neighbor Bill. But today he and his family are active members of our church.

3. Proclamation

The third essential element in winning people to Jesus is *proclamation*. Paul said it is not enough just to spend time with people, or even to build bridges to people by becoming involved in their lives. We must also open our mouths and lovingly, effectively proclaim the gospel. Listen to what he says:

> When I preach the gospel, I cannot boast, for I am compelled to preach. Woe to me if I do not preach the gospel! If I preach voluntarily, I have a reward; if not voluntarily, I am simply discharging the trust committed to me. (9:16–17)

When Paul refers to a "woe" upon him if he does not preach the gospel (you can translate that word *preach* as "proclaim"), he does not mean that he fears punishment if he refuses. Rather, he senses the great responsibility entrusted to him. God had given him the Great Commission to go and make disciples of all nations. In a preceding sentence he says he "would rather die than have anyone deprive" him of the opportunity to freely, without charge, proclaim the gospel to people.

Once while teaching an Evangelism Explosion Leadership Training Clinic in Minneapolis, I noticed an unusually committed lay person who, in sharing the gospel, went far beyond any other volunteer I had ever worked with. Carol was the cook for our meals. She also served us refreshments. During the classes she participated in the training demonstrations. And when it came time for on-the-job training, Carol took off her apron and went out with a visitation team.

My curiosity got the best of me. I had to find out why Carol should be so motivated. So when Carol's team returned to the church, I asked her.

"This is what I'm alive for!" she responded. Then she went on to explain. A few years earlier, she was on her way home from work when a car drove straight at her. As she swerved to avoid a head-on collision, she lost control and her car rolled down an embankment into a lake. Carol managed to escape through one of the windows and floated to the top of the water. But she could not swim. Fortunately, the other driver had stopped. He saw her struggling in the water, dived into the lake and rescued her.

On the first anniversary of the accident, Carol invited the other driver out to lunch to express again to him her gratitude for rescuing her from the lake. In the ensuing year she had taken Evangelism Explosion training and knew how to share the gospel with her rescuer. Before lunch was over, he had invited Jesus Christ into his life.

"So you see, Pastor," Carol concluded, "I sense that I'm alive for one purpose: to proclaim the gospel of Jesus Christ!"

Carol's motivation was very similar to Paul's. She sensed her God-given responsibility to tell forth the gospel.

An insidious error is being spread throughout our churches. People are saying that Christians need only witness by their friendship, love, caring deeds and exemplary lives. I remember hearing a well-meaning Indian pastor say as much at the 1969 Singapore Congress on Evangelism.

"The church has talked about Christianity for centuries," he said. "I think we have talked about Christ long enough! Let's begin to keep our mouths shut and let our lives point others to Christ."

Part of that Indian pastor's speech was accurate. Our lives must point others to Christ. The other part—that we should close our mouths—was a disastrous contradiction of Christ's command to proclaim this wonderful news to everyone everywhere! Our lips as well as our lives need to proclaim the good news of Jesus. And let us be careful that our lips and lives complement each other!

4. Persuasion

There is a fourth element in winning people to Christ. It is *persuasion*. Having stated that he was under a commission to proclaim the gospel, Paul went on to add most emphatically that he must do so winsomely, persuasively, successfully. Notice his repeated use of the little word *win*:

> Though I am free and belong to no man, I make myself a slave to everyone, to *win* as many as possible. To the Jews I became like a Jew, to *win* the Jews. To those under the law I became like one under the law, . . . so as to *win* those under the law. To those not having the law I became like one not having the law, . . . so as to *win* those not having the law. To the weak I became weak, to *win* the weak. I have become all things to all men so that by all possible means I might save some. (9:19–22)

Then, lest his readers not understand his clear purpose to witness in such a way as to persuade people and win them to faith in Christ, Paul adds:

> Do you not know that in a race all the runners run, but only one gets the prize? Run in such a way as to get the prize. (9:24)

In other words, Paul is saying that anyone can run, but the important thing is to win! Anyone can in some manner—poorly or otherwise—witness, but the important thing and the real purpose is to persuade people—to win them to faith in Christ! The chief goal of proclaiming the gospel is to see people believe—to see them won to Christ!

Unfortunately, too many Christians are content to witness without winning anyone to Christ. They rationalize something like this: "God doesn't require that we be successful as long as we are faithful." Have you ever heard that well-meant but dreadfully erroneous half-truth? I have heard it shouted from pulpits and taught in Sunday school classes—in conservative, evangelical, Bible-believing churches, no less!

As false as Baal

This effort to take away the embarrassment of a barren church or the guilt of a sterile life is as false today as the ancient teachings of Baal ever were. To be heretical, a statement does not have to be totally contrary to Scripture. It can be a nice-sounding half-truth. And that is exactly what this seemingly innocent statement is: a half-truth.

Half-truths like this usually have some biblical basis, but too often the Scripture used is either taken out of context or otherwise twisted in its interpretation. For example, to support this half-truth some teachers misuse the parable of the talents (Matthew 25:14–30). The master, returning home to settle accounts with his servants, praised the first two with the words, "Well done, good and faithful servant! You have been faithful with a few things; I will put you in charge of many things. Come and share your master's happiness."

Usually the preacher or teacher quotes the words and then goes on to reason, "The master in the parable did not say, 'Well done, good and *successful* servant.' He said, 'Good and *faithful* servant.'" The argument sounds plausible until we look at Jesus' parable more closely. Then it becomes clear that the two servants were praised precisely because they had been successful. Each of them had doubled the money entrusted to him. And the third servant was sternly rebuked and punished because he had not been successful in increasing his master's money. In other words, if we are truly faithful, we will be *successful*, and our success will be rewarded by our heavenly Master.

The dictionary defines success as "a favorable or satisfactory result or outcome." In speaking of success the Bible uses several synonyms. On the battlefield, success means being "victorious" (1 Kings 22:15). When it is the building of a temple for God, it is "progress" (Ezra 5:8). When it is the work of a wise administrator, the term is "prospered" (Daniel 6:28). The Proverbs measure success with a string of equivalent words ranging from prolonged life and prosperity to favor and a good name, from bodily health and nourishment of the bones to overflowing barns and brimming vats (Proverbs 3:1–10).

God wants winners

Paul employs the word *win* to describe success in proclaiming the gospel (1 Corinthians 9:19–22). Since we also are speaking of proclaiming the gospel, that is the term we shall use.

The Bible clearly teaches that God wants—no, He expects!—every Christian to win people to faith in Christ Jesus. God desires that Christians not only witness but that they actually win those to whom they witness.

A fisherman does not cast a net or drop a hook into the water simply to get it wet. His goal is to catch fish! A farmer does not plant seed just for something to do after plowing season. He expects to harvest a crop! And Paul adds that runners do not run simply for the exercise and boxers do not box just to beat the air. They run with the hope of winning! Likewise, we must proclaim the gospel—we must witness—with the clear-cut purpose of winning people to faith in Christ. We should not be content until we successfully bear fruit. We should not be satisfied until we win people to Christ and see them enfolded in the church as responsible, growing, Spirit-filled, reproducing disciples.

God longs to see men and women, youth and children, won to His kingdom. He yearns to see them loosed from the chains of sin and death. He waits for us to capture them for Christ and His gentle mastery. He rejoices over each one that we bring into the glorious liberty enjoyed by the children of God. Will we determine by His grace and enabling power to win people for His kingdom and glory?

Maybe you have agreed with me this far, but you say, "I just do not know how to win people to Jesus. I want to successfully proclaim the good news, but how do I persuade those to whom I speak?"

If that is your problem, you are not alone! Thousands of others are similarly frustrated. Help is on the way! And that brings us to the fifth essential element in winning people to Christ:

5. Preparation

As someone has said, if you fail to prepare, you prepare to fail. The reason so many Christians fail in their efforts to win people to Christ is that no one has prepared them for the job. They have heard great sermons on witnessing. They have seen films that motivated them to share their faith. They have attended classes on how to tell others about Jesus. They have watched—enviously—evangelists at work. But no one has taken them by the hand and trained them to win people to Christ.

Preparation—training—is the key! Preparation, following Jesus' model—is the key!

But first, look closely at what Paul says about preparing for a foot race or a boxing match. These words could be the most important in this whole book about personal evangelism! If you can grasp what Paul, inspired by the Holy Spirit, is saying, and if you will apply his words in your life, you will find they will unlock for you—and the people whose lives you touch—a great new future. It is the secret of a fulfilling ministry beyond your wildest dreams.

Here is Paul's statement:

> Everyone who competes in the games goes into strict training. They do it to get a crown that will not last; but we do it to get a crown that will last forever. (9:25)

Paul says that just as a runner or boxer goes into "strict training," so the person who wants to win people to Christ must also go into strict training.

The University of Nebraska Cornhuskers ended the 80s decade with the winningest record in college football. That was no accident. They are also known to have the finest weight-lifting, body-building program of any college team. I have been in their training room. One of their mottos is "No pain, no gain." Long before the first kickoff—in fact, all during the summer months—the players prepare themselves for the football season. They know from experience that to win they must prepare. They must train, and train hard.

When Mike Tyson lost his heavyweight crown, sports analysts stated that his fight was not lost in the ring but in the training gym. In winning people to Christ it is the same. Christians succeed or fail not in the confrontation but because of the training they had or did not have.

Annie

One day Annie, a woman in our church in her 60s, approached me.

"Pastor Tom," she began, "I've been working in the church nursery for years and have just retired. I think it's time for me to be trained in evangelism. I'm planning to enlist in the Evangelism Explosion course next semester."

The next semester Annie registered, purchased her materials and started on the homework assignments. Each week she faithfully studied the lesson, recited the material to her trainer, went out for on-the-job practice with her team of three. Little by little she was developing into an effective communicator of the gospel. Before long she reported her first success in evangelism. Soon she was reporting conversions outside of the weekly class time. Eventually she was training others.

Then the day came when I fielded a tough assignment. I had a telephone call from the hospital. A man by the name of Jack reported that his wife was dying. Although he was a believer, his wife was not. Jack had never been able to lead his wife to Christ. Would I come before it was too late?

I rushed to the hospital only to find Jack's wife in a coma. I left with my mission unfulfilled. But a little while later Jack called me again. The doctor said he could bring his wife out of the coma one more time. Jack wanted me to be on 24-hour stand-by. My schedule just then, however, prevented such a commitment.

"I'll tell you what, Jack," I said. "I have just the person. Her name is Annie. I will alert her to the situation. She will be near her telephone the next 24 hours. When your wife regains consciousness, call Annie. She'll go to the hospital at once."

The next day Jack called, and Annie responded. In a short while, as Annie spoke with her, Jack's wife gave her heart to Jesus. Amazingly, the woman continued to live for two or three days. Her family gathered around her to read the Scriptures, to pray and to sing praises to the Lord. The Sunday after his wife went home to be with the Lord, Jack and his entire family were in church. And they have attended faithfully ever since.

"I decided that any church that could lead my wife to the Lord like that was the church where I wanted to belong," Jack told me. In fact, Jack was so impressed at Annie's ability to witness that he himself signed up to be trained in evangelism.

6. Prize

We come to the sixth and final consideration in First Corinthians 9: the *prize*. Athletic contests were common in the Greek world. The Corinthian Christians to whom Paul addressed his letter were well aware of the Isthmian games. Second only to the Olympics held at Athens, they took place every three years. Doubtless it is from those games that Paul drew his analogy of running:

> Do you not know that in a race all the runners run, but only one gets the prize? Run in such a way as to get the prize. . . . They do it to get a crown that will not last; but we do it to get a crown that will last forever. (9:24–25)

The prizes given to Greek athletes were crowns of pine or olive branches. When worn home they were cause for great pride and rejoicing. But as they hung on the wall or were placed in a trophy case, they soon withered. Their glory did not last!

In contrast Paul exhorted the Corinthian Christians to labor for a prize that would last forever! What exactly was the crown to which he referred? Was it a gold crown studded with diamonds?

Hardly. The Bible tells us of only two things that will last forever: the Word of God, which shall never pass away, and the souls of men and women, which are eternal. I believe the prize for which Paul exhorted the Corinthians to strive and that which would bring them great joy in heaven was *people*—people won to the Master. That was the crown they could some day lay at Jesus' feet.

In his first letter to the church at Thessalonica, Paul says as much: "What is our hope, our joy, or the crown in which we will glory in the presence of our Lord Jesus when he comes? Is it not you? Indeed, you are our glory and joy" (1 Thessalonians 2:19). Paul says his prize, his crown that will last forever, is the Thessalonian and Corinthian believers whom he had a part in winning to Jesus Christ.

So Paul began First Corinthians 9 by saying that his work was *people*, and now he ends the chapter stating that his prize is those *people* when they are won to Christ and one day meet him in heaven.

When you get to heaven, after you have spent a trillion years looking at Jesus and worshiping Him in all His glory, who else do you want to meet? Moses? Elijah? David? John the Baptist? Paul?

The first two persons I want to meet are Merv Roselle and Mom! Why them? Because it was

Merv Roselle who proclaimed the gospel that night in 1942 in Nyack, New York, when I came in faith to Jesus Christ. And it was Mom who prayed with me to invite Jesus into my life as my personal Savior. Yes, I want to meet them and thank them for their part in winning me to Jesus Christ. I suppose you could say that I will be their prize, their crown of rejoicing in the presence of the Lord.

I ask you: When Jesus comes, will you receive any prizes for your endeavors here on earth to win people to Jesus? Will you have any eternal crowns to lay at Jesus' feet?

In eternity will you look back at the end of your race and see a beautifully decorated home, a manicured yard, a successful business, a list of educational accomplishments, some sports trophies, a big bank account? Like the withered pine and olive wreaths of Greek competition, all those material things will have perished.

Or will you rejoice as you meet those who have gone on before you and others who may follow you through heaven's gates—ones who are there because you took time to witness to them? On planet earth they were *people* in your network of relationships. And you *penetrated* their busy little "world," building bridges of friendship to them. Then when the opportunity presented itself, you *proclaimed* to them the most wonderful news they could ever hear. In the power of the Holy Spirit you *persuaded* them to trust Christ as Savior and Lord. Yes, those months of *preparation* and training were tough! But your *prize*, received at heaven's gate, makes it all worthwhile.

What joy, what glory as you behold your eternal "crowns"! What an honor to place them at the feet of King Jesus!

Recall God's word to Daniel, "Those who are wise will shine like the brightness of the heavens, and those who lead many to righteousness, like the stars forever and ever" (12:3). May you be one of those wise, bright "stars" surrounded by your trophies of God's grace!

Study Questions

1 Corinthians 9

1. According to verses 19–24, what is the race Paul is seeking to win and that we should also endeavor to win?
2. If someone were to ask you what your purpose or mission in life is, how—in one sentence—would you define it?
3. According to verses 16–17, what motivates Paul to proclaim the gospel? What other factors might motivate a Christian to witness?
4. When it comes to evangelism, what groups of people in your community are being neglected? The poor? Elderly? Unwed mothers? Single

parents? Prostitutes? Prisoners? The extremely rich? An ethnic group?

5. What practical steps might your church take to penetrate with an effective witness one or all of these groups?

6. How would you respond to this statement: "God doesn't expect Christians to win people to Christ, just to sow the seed and to witness, since He ultimately is responsible for the results"?

7. How do you apply "Everyone who competes in the games goes into strict training" (verse 25) to the business of soul-winning? What is your church doing to apply this principle?

8. When your life is done, what of eternal value are you planning to lay at Jesus' feet?

CHAPTER 8

Heralding Good News

2 Timothy 1, 2

BETH HAD BEEN APPLYING herself assiduously to the 16-week Evangelism Explosion training course at Crystal Evangelical Free Church in Minneapolis. She had learned the basic gospel outline; she had memorized Bible verses to back it up. Beth was also evidencing some definite progress as she practiced sharing her faith with others.

Then came her first, nervous for-real presentation to a woman who needed Christ. In spite of Beth's "stumbling" delivery, as she later described it, the woman to whom she was witnessing invited Jesus into her life. Beth should have been elated.

Instead, she had second thoughts about the whole process. "As I drove home from that presentation," she remembers, "I told the Lord I was going to quit E.E. I'd been a Christian 20 years and I didn't need some 'canned' outline for sharing the gospel. If God wanted me to witness, people would ask me about my faith and He would give me the words. Period!"

Period.

But within a few minutes Beth had calmed down. "Lord," she continued contritely as she drove, "You know how I feel. If You really did tell me to be in E.E. and You want me to continue, You're going to have to give me the motivation. I can't do it without You."

The words were hardly out of her mouth when barely two blocks in front of her Beth saw a pick-up skid across the street into a telephone pole.

"I'm a respiratory therapist and teach CPR as part of my job," Beth says, "so I pulled into a parking place near the crash and went over to see if I could help. Several motorists had already pulled the man from the truck, laying him on the sidewalk. But no one was doing anything more. I pushed through the gathering crowd and knelt by the injured man. As I questioned him about his pain, I also quickly checked his pulse. It was palpable but weak.

"As the moments ticked by, I reviewed in my mind the steps of CPR. If the man was bleeding internally and should lose his pulse, I knew it would be necessary to begin cardiopulmonary resuscitation without a moment's hesitation.

Her crisis was over

"The heartbeat continued, the paramedics arrived and my crisis was over," Beth continues. "Back in my car, I was very thankful the man had lived. I thought back to my CPR training and how tiring it was to learn. Over and over we did the same routines until they were second nature to us. But all the practice had been worth it! I could have performed CPR at that crash without hesitation.

"Suddenly, I realized God had answered my prayer about E.E. motivation! The memorized and often-practiced E.E. outline was really no different than the CPR routine I had practiced over and over. With CPR, I was ready to save a person from physical death any time I was needed. With E.E., I was equipped through the Holy Spirit's power to rescue a person from eternal death."

Thoroughly convinced of the necessity to learn a clear, concise, biblical gospel presentation so as to be "always ... prepared" with "a reason for the hope" that she had (1 Peter 3:15), Beth flew through the next 10 weeks of training. Since then she has become a trainer of others and has gone on to be certified as an E.E. lay teacher/trainer.

What Beth learned that day as she drove home from her first "live" encounter, scores of other Christians have learned. Some are using the "Roman Road," others the "Four Spiritual

Laws," still others the "Bridge Illustration." But one thing they all have in common is a basic outline with Scriptures and illustrations to bring another person to an understanding of God's plan of salvation through Christ Jesus.

Some Christians advocate a more spontaneous approach to sharing the good news. They caricature the above gospel presentations as artificial or as "sales pitches." They feel all they need to do is get people converted, filled with the Spirit and motivated by divine love, then send them out to extemporize about the way of salvation whenever a situation presents itself. Regrettably, it does not usually happen that way. Jesus seems to have felt it was important to prepare His disciples. He took three years to equip them for sharing the good news.

We have good biblical precedent for using a clear, concise, practiced gospel presentation when we witness. For convenience I shall use the words *formulating, learning, equipping, multiplying* in this chapter as I discuss "heralding the good news."

1. Formulating

God is a God of order, design and structure. In creating us in His image He has given us minds that think in an orderly way and that reason systematically. If, therefore, we want to understand and to communicate the gospel clearly, it is essential that we formulate it into a statement that has order, design and structure.

In his second letter to Timothy, his spiritual "son," Paul makes several references to the gospel. He refers to the gospel as a body of truth that had taken some form or pattern. This gospel was heard, heralded, taught, entrusted, kept and suffered for:

> Do not be ashamed to testify about our Lord, or ashamed of me his prisoner. But join with me in suffering for the gospel.... Of this gospel I was appointed a herald and an apostle and a teacher.... What you heard from me, keep as the pattern of sound teaching, with faith and love in Christ Jesus. Guard the good deposit that was entrusted to you. (1:8–14)

Michael Green, in his classic work *Evangelism in the Early Church* (Eerdmans), gives us some thoughtful insight into how the early church took the saving news of the gospel and formulated it into statements that could be learned and shared with others. He writes:

> It was no ordinary news that rocked Palestine around the year A.D. 30. It was no mere message about a carpenter-teacher who had been executed under the Roman procurator. It was nothing less than the joyful announcement of the long awaited

Messianic salvation when God had come to the rescue of a world in need. Small surprise, then, that the content of their message became known as the *euaggelion*— the good news.

The gospel had a recognizable shape and content . . . There was some sort of "pattern of sound words," and this proved a useful springboard for the memories of the evangelists: it did not serve as a straightjacket, inhibiting all imagination and initiative on their part. (pages 49, 63, 70)

C. H. Dodd and a large number of other historians of the early church period agree with Michael Green that such a "pattern of sound words" was, in fact, a creedal formula that reduced the saving truth of the gospel into a systematic, understandable, easily-expressed statement. Moreover, these historians believe that such a statement of faith was not intended to be recited like the Apostles' Creed in worship services, but learned and then shared in various witnessing situations.

A gospel outline

Based on what I have quoted above, Green evidently sees a reference to such a creedal statement or outline of the gospel in Second Timothy 1:13:

What you heard from me, keep as the pattern of sound teaching, with faith and love
in Christ Jesus.

The same idea comes through even more clearly in some of the other translations of that
verse:

Hold fast the form of sound words which
thou hast heard of me. (King James Version)

Retain the standard of sound words which
you have heard from me. (New American
Standard Version)

Keep before you an outline of the sound
teaching which you heard from me. (New
English Bible)

The key word is the one variously translated
"pattern," "form," "standard," "outline." In his
Expository Dictionary of New Testament Words,
W. E. Vine defines it as "outline, pattern, sketch
or form." It is derived from the Greek word
meaning "form" or "mold." Vine says, "The
metaphor is that of a cast or frame into which
molten material is poured so as to take shape"
(page 124).

We might say the "outline" or "pattern of
sound words" to which Paul referred was a
kind of mold into which saving truth had been

poured. It gave form, order, system and clarity of expression so that the communicator as well as the receiver might easily understand the message.

A tested formula

The Evangelism Explosion gospel presentation is an example. It has been thoughtfully formulated both from Scripture and experience. Over a period of years it has been tested and refined. By now it has been effectively used to bring salvation to tens of thousands of men, women, youth and children spanning every continent of earth. It is not a magic wand to be waved over a community or church in hopes that something extraordinary will happen. Rather, it is a tool. Like any tool, it requires a degree of effort, skill and persistence on the part of the user.

Evangelism Explosion compares its gospel presentation to the human body. The outline is the skeleton; the Scripture references are flesh and muscle; the illustrations, hair and clothing. The basic skeleton, which gives the presentation structure and form, remains always the same, but hair style and dress will vary depending on the person making the presentation and the circumstances.

Before I learned E.E.'s gospel presentation, I was reticent to share the gospel person-to-person. There were many unknowns. I did not know exactly how to get into the gospel. Once in, I was not sure what I should include. And if I got that far, I did not know how to bring the other person to a solid commitment. Now that I have learned a carefully formulated, well-tested outline, I am at all times comfortable in sharing the good news with those I meet.

So a gospel outline is a very useful tool for formulating saving truth into a clear, systematic message that both sharer and sinner can easily understand.

2. Learning

Once a concise, clear, biblical gospel outline has been put together, it must be learned. The outline must become fixed in our hearts and minds. It must be committed to memory so that at any time we are ready to share the good news with others. That is why Paul said to Timothy:

> What you heard from me, keep as the pattern of sound teaching . . . Guard the good deposit that was entrusted to you . . . (1:13–14)

Michael Green also mentions in his book that at first there was an "oral period when the good news was not written down but passed on by word of mouth in the market place, bazaars and wine shops of that day. . . . The story was so vital to the early church, however, that they had at all costs to preserve it."

Paul exhorts Timothy, therefore, to commit to memory and keep the truth of the gospel as it was passed on to him.

Most Christians do not share the gospel with family, friends and associates because of fear. The reason they are afraid is that they are unprepared. They have never learned a clear, concise, biblical way to present this vital message.

An outline committed to memory will go a long way in overcoming fear. It is the unknown that prompts our fear, tying our tongues, short-circuiting our thought processes. We are afraid we cannot lead naturally into the subject of the gospel. And if we should get that far, we are afraid we will not know what to say next. We fear we will not have answers to the questions the other person may ask us, or not know how to bring the person to a place of decision or not know what to do if the person turns us down. How wonderful it is to be liberated from these crippling fears! A well-learned gospel presentation will equip us to handle all such difficult situations—and more!

Perhaps you are thinking, "He sounds convincing, but I have the worst memory in the world. I could never memorize a gospel presentation!" If that is your problem, I can identify with you. My memory is like a sieve. If I had to earn a living using only my memory, I would be a life-time pauper.

The fact is, most people I talk to about learning to share their faith respond the same way. But I have seen hundreds—no, *thousands*—of fellow believers surprise themselves by learning a clear, simple gospel presentation.

Jim was one

When I moved from Hong Kong to Omaha and prepared to launch an evangelism ministry at our church, I approached an elderly man in the congregation, attempting to enlist him in our first semester of training.

"Jim," I said, "I want you to prayerfully consider coming into our Evangelism Explosion training that starts the first of September."

"Thank you for thinking of me, Pastor," Jim responded. "But I have my own way of introducing people to Jesus Christ. At my age I think it's a little late to make a change. And, to be perfectly honest with you, I don't think I could learn all that material."

As badly as I wanted to recruit Jim, I could clearly see it would not help to say anything further. His mind was made up. He was quite satisfied to open his presentation with two questions borrowed from E.E. Then he would search his pockets until he found one of his little gospel booklets, pull up a chair next to his "prospect" and begin reading the tract word-by-word.

On the eve of our E.E. enlistment banquet something unusual happened to Jim. He had a dream. The next day a very disturbed Jim shared his dream with me.

"Pastor," he said, "in my dream I stopped at a filling station for some gas. As I pulled up to one of the self-service pumps, another driver stopped right across from me. He was friendly, so after we exchanged a few words, I asked him the two questions about eternal life. When he gave me the wrong answers, I asked him if I could share with him some wonderful news.

"When the fellow agreed, I looked through all my pockets for one of my booklets. They were all gone! In desperation, I asked if he would wait a minute while I drove home to get a gospel booklet. But as I pulled out of the station, I noticed in my mirror that he also was driving away. It was too late!

"Pastor," Jim concluded, "do you still have room in that evangelism class? I've gotta learn to share the gospel without depending any longer on a printed booklet."

Of course I found a place for Jim. And to his great surprise, Jim not only learned the presentation but became a star witness and a trainer of other personal evangelists. Jim never missed a semester of training until the day he died.

Even the funeral counted

I cannot forget Jim's funeral. As his body lay silently in state as the mourners passed by, everyone saw on the lapel of his dark suit the gold two-question-mark pin of E.E. It reminded me of Jim's readiness at all times to share his faith.

Senior Pastor Bob Thune, as he spoke to those who had come to the funeral, used Jim's favorite presentation of the gospel. Jim would have jumped for joy at the response. Ten of his friends gave their hearts to Christ that day!

Most of us have a much better memory than we are willing to acknowledge. Our memories came as a birthday gift—an extremely valuable gift. Memory is as essential to our intellectual process as breathing is to our physical life. Memory must be used, developed, trained. There are some principles that can help us cultivate a surprisingly good memory.

One of these principles that we all unconsciously use to help us remember important pieces of information is *association*. There are "links" or "pegs" that remind us of harder-to-remember details. For instance, in my daily prayer time I use as an outline an acronym someone taught me taken from the Bible book of Acts: *A*doration, *C*onfession, *T*hanksgiving, *S*upplication. Simple—and good!

In our E.E. classes I teach my students to learn the outline of the introduction with the acronym SCOPE. Assisted by this easy-to-remember association, they cover *S*ecular life, *C*hurch background, *O*ur church, *P*ersonal/church testimony, *E*ternal life questions.

Another memorization principle is *repetition*. I have discovered that if I repeat something over and over—say, 30 times—and if I will review it over and over—say, every day for four or five months, it begins to become a part of me.

I did this with language study. Vietnamese is one of the most difficult languages in the world. Probably the hardest thing about it, at least for Americans, is its tonal nature. Simply by the speaker's voice inflection, a given word can have five totally different meanings. For example, the word *ma* can mean "mother," "but," "rice shoot," "horse" or "devil." Multiply all those meanings by the number of words in a given sentence, and the possibility for gaffes is astounding!

How did I remember to raise or drop my voice at the proper place for the meaning I wanted? Repetition. Over and over I repeated basic sentences with the proper inflection until they were second nature to me. After several months, the inflection became almost automatic. Unconsciously I began raising or dropping the pitch of my voice, like singing a tune. In time I found myself speaking that difficult language accurately and smoothly—because I had repeated the words and phrases over and over.

Learning a gospel outline with appropriate verses and illustrations is possible for anyone who will follow this same principle of repetition.

Material must be used

There is a third learning principle in addition

to association and repetition. People remember something that they *use at once and regularly*. I saw this principle also at work in my language study. In high school I studied French for two years. But I remember very little of it simply because I never had French-speaking friends here in the United States with whom I could talk.

But in Vietnam, I was surrounded by Vietnamese-speaking people. I had to learn to speak in order to survive! Because I used what I had learned immediately and often, it became part of me. It became so much a part of me that today, more than 15 years after I had to leave Vietnam—I cannot forget the language. It is engraved deep in my memory.

There is still a fourth principle that will help us learn a gospel presentation. It is what we call *incremental learning*. By that we mean learning a little bit at a time over an extended period rather than trying to learn it all in one sitting.

Someone has observed, "By the yard it's hard; by the inch it's a cinch!" If I tried to move from the first floor of my home to the second in one giant step, it would be impossible. But by using the 14 steps called a stairway it is very easy.

All of the above learning methods are employed in Evangelism Explosion training. And as a result, thousands and thousands of people who professed poor memories have mastered the gospel presentation and are leading family, friends and associates to Christ. Friendship evangelism is a reality to these people. It is a part of their everyday life.

There is a divine element

But thus far we have considered only natural, human principles in the task of learning a gospel presentation. There is a divine element that must not be overlooked. It is the inner enabling of the Holy Spirit. And that is precisely what Paul says in Second Timothy 1:14. Having exhorted Timothy to keep what he had heard from Paul as a pattern of sound teaching, he exhorts, "Guard it with the help of the Holy Spirit who lives in us."

Earlier, Jesus had promised His disciples that the Holy Spirit would "teach" them "all things" and "remind" them of "everything" He had said to them (John 14:26). How marvelous it is that we have a divine Prompter within us to help us remember the things we need to share and to give us the power to share these truths clearly and effectively! Do you see why our dependence upon the Holy Spirit is so important?

Let me illustrate it by returning to the metaphor of the human body. A person can have a skeleton, flesh, muscle, hair, and be attractively clothed—and be dead! Without breath he or she is just a corpse! Likewise, there must be the breath of the Holy Spirit to make every gospel presentation alive with relevance, power and conviction.

If a gospel presentation is memorized word-perfect and presented impeccably, but without the anointing of the Holy Spirit, it will be mechanical, dead, ineffective. The sharing of the good news must be in the power of the Holy Spirit or it will be fruitless. As I have said before, the sharing must not simply be dialogue; it must be "tri-alogue"—the participation of the witness, the sinner and the Holy Spirit.

3. Equipping

The third valuable use of a gospel outline is for training. Having trained His disciples for three years, Jesus turned to them and told them to do the same: "Go and make disciples," He said (Matthew 28:19).

In the New Testament use of the word, a disciple was a learning follower. Consider, by way of example, how Jesus' disciples learned to pray.

Prayer was certainly important to the success of Jesus' kingdom. Jesus' disciples had seen Jesus pray often. They had seen the impact of His prayers. They were also aware that John the Baptist had taught his disciples to pray. One day they said to Jesus, "Lord, teach us to pray, just as John taught his disciples to pray" (Luke 11:1).

How did Jesus go about teaching His disciples to pray? He gave them a model prayer. It was not necessarily intended to be a prayer that they would recite in unison every Sunday morning as they worshiped, or every Wednesday evening at the conclusion of their prayer meeting. Rather, it was an outline of the basic elements of prayer. In training His disciples, Jesus used an outline that they could learn and reproduce in their own prayer life.

How interesting that Paul used this same methodology in training his disciple Timothy to witness. After charging Timothy to "keep as the pattern of sound teaching" the things he had heard from Paul and to "guard the good deposit that was entrusted to [him]," he went on to add:

> And the things you have heard me say in the presence of many witnesses entrust to reliable men. (2:2)

The gospel outline he had received and learned from Paul, Timothy was now to use in the training of others. How important that Timothy have a transferable tool for training others—one that would convey accurately the saving gospel to his own disciples!

Equipping is essential

It is not enough for a teacher to set forth some general principles and a broad strategy of personal evangelism, including a few key Bible verses and some lucid illustrations. From personal experience I can state that it is essential—as well as biblical—to train learners to commit to memory a well-formulated gospel presentation such as the one used in Evangelism Explosion. That is our only assurance that they will be indeed well-prepared. It is our only assurance that their message will be, in fact, the good news set forth in the New Testament and not some watered-down, incomplete facsimile.

Did you ever play that group game where one person whispers a message in the ear of the person sitting next, who in turn passes it to the next until it has made the rounds? Not usually is there much relation between what the last person received and the message the first person whispered.

When that happens in an evening of group games, it is funny. But when it takes place in evangelism it is tragic.

That is why Evangelism Explosion insists that each trainee memorize the basic outline and Scriptures. That is why E.E. gives its teachers detailed notes and requires that each teacher be carefully trained and certified. E.E. is concerned that in this "life-and-death" ministry, the message be totally consistent with the Scriptures and presented in a manner best calculated to win the other person to Jesus Christ.

But lest you suppose that E.E. is wooden or mechanical, let me hasten to go on. Although the outline and the Scriptures are carefully memorized for the training sessions, we encourage each trainee to be flexible in, and to personalize, his or her actual sharing encounters. That is where the Holy Spirit's help that Paul refers to in Second Timothy 1:14 is so crucial.

Even in its training situations, E.E. encourages trainees to tailor the presentation to fit the other individual's special need. If, for example, the person is works-oriented, the witness should flesh out the grace part of the outline. If the person evidences loose morals, the witness will expand on the sin part of the presentation.

But to maintain accuracy and quality, E.E. requires that everyone learn, train from and teach the same basic outline. Then as they move out into their circle of relationships, they learn with the help of God's Spirit to make the appropriate adaptations for each differing personality and situation.

The Holy Spirit provided an opening

Andrew, a Chinese Christian businessman whom I met in Manila, later wrote me about his experience with Evangelism Explosion as he had dinner with a Manila attorney and his wife.

Our dinner lasted for three hours. For the first hour and a half I listened with bewilderment as these two shared with me their arguments. For instance, they concluded that God must have created evil as well as good. If God created only good, then humans are greater than God because we can create evil, which God cannot. I was continuously praying to God for direction.

I had about decided it was useless to try to present the gospel to this couple when the attorney suddenly said he was looking for someone to explain the truth to him. He even repeated the statement. That was my opening! After an hour of Evangelism Explosion, both of them prayed to receive Christ. They were both very happy. They said they will remember that night forever. The attorney added that this is the first time anyone had explained to him the real meaning of *Jesus* and *believing*.

Praise God! And praise God for the E.E. outline!

When Andrew was trained, he learned a gospel outline. He was equipped, ready and effective when God gave him the opportunity to share Christ with his attorney friend and his wife.

4. Multiplying

If the gospel is to be heralded as widely as

Christ intended, if the church is to grow as rapidly as Christ intended, then we His followers must become multipliers.

Multiplication is a universal phenomenon in our world—except for local church membership. People multiply. Animals multiply. Plants multiply. Microbes multiply. But so often a church remains small, its membership stagnant.

The early church, through the first three centuries of the Christian era, multiplied both in membership and in number of churches. God never intended this multiplication to stop. He desires yet that the number of those heralding His good news multiply greatly! Only then will "this gospel of the kingdom . . . be preached in the whole world for a testimony to all nations" (Matthew 24:14).

But how can we multiply the number of good news heralds? Paul gave his disciple Timothy the secret:

> The things you have heard me say in the presence of many witnesses entrust to reliable men who will also be qualified to teach others. (2:2)

Notice the four "generations" of evangelistic reproduction: (1) Paul trained (2)Timothy, who was to (3) train "reliable men" who in turn would (4) train still others. Now if Paul trained just 12 "Timothys"—Silas, Titus, Mark, Epaphras, Luke, Aquila, Priscilla, Gaius, Aristarchus, Philemon, Tertius, Jason, Stephanus, Tychicus, Epaphroditus, Artemas—and each of those 12 reliable people trained 12 others, you would soon, after four generations, have 1,728 good news heralds!

This clearly was Christ's secret of multiplication. After He had trained the "12" He commanded them in turn to make disciples. Every Christian admits to this pattern. Our preachers preach it. People write books about this biblical strategy. But in our generation we do not see it happening very often. Why? I believe it is because most of us have not found a tool to enable us to multiply. That was my problem for many years—20 to be exact.

At last, a "tool"!

I had studied about the principle of training-to-multiply in Bible college. I met Dawson Trotman, founder of the Navigators, and for a week sat at the feet of that master discipler. I read and reread Robert Coleman's book *Master Plan of Evangelism* that magnificently sets forth this biblical strategy. I myself preached sermons and taught seminars challenging other to multiply themselves by equipping disciples for ministry. But the sad fact is that in 20 years I equipped, at most, five reliable men who, in turn, would witness and train others to witness. That was not multiplication. In fact, it could hardly be called addition!

But then, as I have already related, I found a tool. It was a gospel presentation and the New Testament strategy that helped me begin to multiply. No longer for me is this biblical principle of multiplication a dream or an ideal. It has become a reality!

When Mary, one of our Christ Community Church missionaries, was home on furlough, I challenged her to attend our annual leadership training clinic for pastors, missionaries and lay leaders. Not only did Mary attend, but she became convinced that it was more important to train people how to lead others to Christ than it was simply to witness herself. As Mary expressed it, if she returned to Colombia and led 100 people to Christ, she would *add to the church in Colombia. But if she trained 100 people to lead people to Christ, she would multiply* the number of believers in the Colombian churches. As Mary said good-bye to us and flew back to South America, it was with a new goal: to train 100 Colombians to be personal evangelists.

She started by training a handful of "reliable" people. They, in turn, joined her in training others. By the time another four-year term of service was up, Mary had reached her goal of 100 personal evangelists! Thanks to the valuable, biblical outline of E.E., these 100, in turn, are training still other personal evangelists. The church is growing. In fact, it is multiplying!

Mary's testimony reminds me of some other missionaries who discovered this marvelous tool for *formulating, learning, equipping* and *multiplying*. After attending a leadership clinic in Birmingham, Alabama, these enthusiastic European missionaries vowed to "step into lifestyle evangelism" as they returned to their areas of service.

"We are excited," they said, "to think of the possibilities as we work with African students and with French and Belgian churches."

But it was their analogies that really warm my heart.

"We have been working with a hoe," they said; "you have given us a tractor with driving lessons included. We were fishing with a stick and string; you gave us a fishing line, maybe even a net!"

The clinic teacher had simply passed on to them what he had received. Now these heralds of the good news are passing it on to still others.

Study Questions

2 Timothy 1, 2

1. Do you prefer to share the gospel in a spontaneous, unstructured way as the Holy Spirit leads in each situation, to follow a carefully structured format that you have learned beforehand or a balance of the above two approaches?

2. How have you been able to use your approach in sharing the gospel? In what situations? With what results? Are you satisfied with that approach?

3. What approach do you use to train someone else? Approximately how many believers have you had a part in training to share their faith? Do you feel that Christ would have you share in the equipping of others for personal evangelism and how?

4. Do you feel being trained to share your faith and being dependent upon the Holy Spirit to help you share are compatible or contradictory?

5. How do you think Second Timothy 2:2 applies to personal evangelism and, in practical, effective terms, how can the church fulfill this application?

CHAPTER 9

Making Reproducing Disciples

John 4

"MY NAME IS EDMUND," announced the visitor at the Kowloon Tong Alliance Church where I was pastor. "I'm an optometrist here in Hong Kong."

"I am pleased to meet you, Edmund," I replied as I shook the man's hand. "What was it that brought you to our church today?"

A blip of pain crossed Edmund's face, and he grew more serious. "Well," he answered, "I'm not a Christian, but my father was. He died last week in Manila in an elevator accident. We brought his body back to Hong Kong. My family are all Christians except me, so I brought them in my car to your church."

I invited Edmund and his family to stay after the worship service for our visitor reception. There I introduced Edmund to Judy. As I did so I mentioned the background information Edmund had volunteered.

"I'm sorry about your father, Edmund," Judy sympathized. "My dad died recently, too. But it's all right; he's in heaven."

"How can you be sure of that?" Edmund wanted to know.

"Well, the Bible tells us we can know for sure. My dad did. I do. And you can know for sure that you will go to heaven." Then Judy abruptly changed the subject. "Say, I need some new contact lenses. If I come by your place, Edmund, can you take care of me?"

A few days later, as he was fitting Judy for her lenses, Edmund asked again how she could be certain her dad was in heaven. Judy offered to bring her evangelism team to his home, where she could explain to him her confidence without taking time from his other clients.

Twice Judy's team visited Edmund—without much success. So Judy asked if she could bring Edmund to my home for another try. She would invite a doctor friend who was also active in our evangelism training ministry.

Knowing that Edmund had already heard the gospel twice, I suggested we modify the usual strategy. "This time, why don't we simply share with Edmund how Christ has worked in each of our lives?"

"I'm ready! I'm convinced!"

Edmund came. In the middle of the third testimony, he excitedly stood to his feet. "I'm
ready!" he exclaimed. "I'm convinced! God has
spoken to me through what you've been
saying."

We joined hands in a circle under the ceiling
fan and led Edmund in a simple prayer. He
began attending church regularly. He joined
our Discovery Class for new believers. Ultimately he enrolled in our Evangelism Explosion training.

Not too long after that, Donna and I moved
from Hong Kong. One day in Omaha the
phone rang. To my surprise, it was Edmund.
"What are you doing in the United States?" I
wanted to know.

"Well, since you left Hong Kong, I've continued to be involved in evangelism," Edmund
explained. "In fact, I have led 26 people to
Christ. And now I'm on my way to Fort
Lauderdale to be trained as a teacher/trainer
so I can continue the evangelism ministry you
started in Hong Kong."

How exciting it was to see this disciple
reproducing other disciples! And that is exactly
what Christ commanded His disciples to do.
"Go and make disciples of all nations," He said
(Matthew 28:19).

In evangelical circles, great emphasis is
placed upon the word *decision*. One of the great

evangelistic magazines and one of the most popular radio and TV programs take their names from this emphasis. Although it is true that we need to bring people to a place of decision, we must do much more. We are under orders to nurture and equip new believers for discipleship.

But what exactly is a disciple? At our church we define a disciple as a learning follower. We aim to bring each disciple to the place where he or she is a spiritually minded, functionally mature, biblically literate, reproducing member of the local church. We place special emphasis upon the reproducing aspect because every Christian, as Navigators founder Dawson Trotman put it, "is born to reproduce."

In John 4 we find a classic lesson on how to make disciples Jesus' way—especially how to make reproducing disciples. This often-read chapter with its story of Jesus and the Samaritan woman at the well begins on the theme of disciple-making:

> The Pharisees heard that Jesus was gaining and baptizing more disciples than John. (4:1)

Then we have described in detail for us Jesus' making of one disciple—a reproducing disciple who, from the standpoint of reproduction, may have put to shame at that point in time Jesus' other disciples. As Jesus models for us the way to make a disciple, three important facets of the process stand out: *preevangelism, presentation* of the gospel and *priorities.*

1. Preevangelism

Obviously, Jesus' concern as He encountered the Samaritan woman at the well in Sychar was her salvation—her conversion from a sinful to a righteous life, her preparation for an eternity in heaven rather than one in hell. But before Jesus made any effort to present the gospel to the unnamed woman, He made certain the "climate" was as favorable as possible. He endeavored to put the woman in a frame of mind that would make her receptive to His salvation message. We call this preevangelism.

Overcoming natural barriers

Christ first found it necessary to overcome natural barriers. In His discussion with the Samaritan, Jesus had to surmount three such obstacles that most people today would consider difficult.

There was the *cultural* difference between Jews and Samaritans. The woman said to Jesus,

> You are a Jew and I am a Samaritan woman. How can you ask me for a drink? (4:9)

Cultural differences can be barriers or

bridges, depending on how we handle them. I mentioned earlier that I gained a hearing as a foreign missionary in Vietnam by learning the language, adapting to the culture, eating the food and living voluntarily in that war-ravished land.

The Samaritan woman's question implied not only the cultural difference but a *gender* difference as well. Jesus was a man. She was a woman. The gender difference was accentuated by the woman's loose morals. Jesus allowed neither consideration to keep Him from speaking to this spiritually needy woman. In the public openness of the village well, He witnessed to her.

Many evangelism teachers insist that we avoid one-to-one witness to a person of the opposite sex. But some of my best encounters have been with women. I have shared Christ with women sitting beside me on planes. Whenever it is to be a private encounter, however, I make sure I have two other evangelism team members with me.

There may be physical difficulties, too

Jesus had also to cope with *physical* difficulties. He was tired (4:6), thirsty (4:8) and presumably hungry (4:8). But it often is in the context of difficulty that God does His greatest work. The Psalmist says, "Those who sow in tears/ will reap with songs of joy" (126:5). When the enemy seems to be attacking most

vehemently is when God is about to do something unusual.

Kim was driving home from work one cold,
snowy Thursday afternoon. Three times she
had to stop to scrape ice from her windshield.
As she drove, her thoughts turned to her evening commitment: *We have E.E. tonight, and Pastor Tom never cancels. I'm not sure I want to go out
on a night like this.* But then she recalled a comment by Elisabeth Elliot. During a raging storm
off eastern Massachusetts men of the U.S. Coast
Guard were about to set out on a daring rescue
mission. Asked if it was not foolhardy in face
of so severe a storm, one of the men replied,
"We have to go out; we do not have to come
back."

Kim went out with her team that evening.
Driving to their first appointment, she noticed
the porch light had not been turned on—a sign
those inside had given up on having any
visitors on such a stormy night. Kim was
tempted to turn around and go home. Just then
the porch light went on and someone called
out, "Come in! We didn't think anyone would
be out in this weather!"

At the end of the evening, Kim and her team
returned home rejoicing. They had introduced
a precious person to the Savior!

Not only must natural barriers be overcome
as part of the preevangelism process, but it is
important to see the potential in each individual. Jesus had been busy selecting dis-

ciples (John 1), attending a sizeable wedding at which He had performed His first miracle (John 2), ridding the Temple of its merchants and money changers (also John 2), talking with Nicodemus, an important and very wealthy Pharisee (John 3). Who would be the next prospect to come into His life? A very unlikely person:

> A Samaritan woman came to draw water. (4:7)

Jesus was God Himself enfleshed. He had a busy schedule. As He reached the village of Sychar He was tired and thirsty and hungry. But He had time for one individual, an individual whom no Jewish priest—or any other Jewish man, for that matter—would have spoken to. Jewish men thanked God every day for three things, one of them being that they were not women. Moreover, this woman was a Samaritan, and "Jews do not associate with Samaritans" (4:9). And besides those two counts against her, she was a Samaritan woman of very questionable morals.

But Jesus saw into that Samaritan woman's heart. He knew that His grace could change her. He looked into her future and saw tremendous potential. This Samaritan woman would be the key to reaching all of Sychar with the good news of a Savior.

In disciple-making we must have that same

capacity to see in each individual God brings our way what that person can become by God's grace. We must look by faith into the future and see in the person the potential he or she brings to God and His kingdom.

A visit from Paul Bunyan

A man giving his name as Russ Esch called me at the office to say one of our members, Bill, had suggested he visit me. We made an appointment, and at the agreed-on time Russ walked into my office. I thought I was looking at Paul Bunyan. Another inch and his head would have hit the top of the door frame. He almost had to turn sideways to get his broad, muscular shoulders through the passage.

Unshaven, reeking of alcohol, shifty-eyed and rather nervous to be face-to-face with a clergyman, Russ nevertheless told me of his checkered background. He drove rigs cross-country. Every truck stop was for him a round of bars, women, drugs, porn movies and rock videos. And then something unusual happened.

"Pastor, while I was watching one of those rock videos, I saw Satan and some of his demons coming toward me. But an angel of light stepped in between us to protect me. The angel told me there were two men who were going to help me. One would tell me how to become a Christian and the other how to grow. I didn't know where to look for those two men. The only Christian I knew was Bill, my insurance agent. So I called him, and Bill sent me to you."

Then Russ Esch added something really weird. "The other day I tried to look up the meaning of my name in a dictionary. The closest any word came to Esch was *eschatology*. The dictionary said it meant the doctrine of future things and that these things were dealt with in the book of Revelation. Do you have any idea what God is trying to say to me?"

"Russ," I answered, "I *know* what God is trying to tell you. First, He has a great future for you. Second, the book of Revelation, chapter 3, verse 20 will tell you how to get started." Together we read the words of Jesus in that verse: "Here I am! I stand at the door and knock. If anyone hears my voice and opens the door, I will come in and eat with him, and he with me."

I told Russ that Jesus had been speaking to him and knocking on his heart's door through the experiences he had just been through. For an hour I shared with him the gospel. As he and I knelt for prayer there in the office, something divine and dynamic took place in his life.

"Now," Russ continued, "who's the second person who is going to tell me how to grow?"

"I know just the man," I responded. "His name is Chuck. Let me call him and get the two of you together." Before Russ left the office, the men had arranged to meet and get started.

Not long ago, just a year after his conversion,

Russ walked into my office. I hardly recognized him. He had been delivered from drugs, alcohol and loose living. He quit driving cross-country and was working for a company whose range was local so Russ could have quality time with his family. Russ's wife, seeing the dramatic change in her husband, had also received Christ. Over his CB radio Russ was witnessing to fellow truckers. If he encountered pornographic literature, he would pull out his Bible and memorize Scripture.

As we talked, Russ indicated his desire to be baptized and to sign up for training in Evangelism Explosion so he would know how to bring others to a place of commitment. He was also thinking about writing his testimony in a tract and starting an evangelism and discipleship ministry for truckers.

Building bridges of friendship

Having seen the potential in an individual, it is important next to build bridges of friendship. Unfortunately, most Christians do not have many close non-Christian friends. When they were converted they took literally the admonition to ". . . come out from them/ and be separate" (2 Corinthians 6:17). All those former relationships that might have served as bridges for sharing the gospel have been burned behind them. By the same token, Christians brought up in the church have chosen their friends from among fellow believers.

Jesus was a friend of "sinners" (Matthew 11:19). He ate with them. He reached out to them wherever He traveled. Sometimes He did favors for them; this time he asked a favor:

Will you give me a drink? (John 4:7)

Someone has suggested that before we can win people to Jesus Christ we must win them to ourselves. Sharing the gospel is a very personal matter. We are probing the most intimate, private areas of the other person's life. So we must first earn that person's trust and build some measure of friendship.

How do we do that? Well, we can join a tennis club. We can become involved in the PTA. We can volunteer to referee or coach in the Little League. We can take some courses at the local community college. We can go to the same hair stylist each time. Or shop at the supermarket during the slow hours so as to build a friendship with one of the cashiers. And there are the neighbors. Could you volunteer to feed a neighbor's pets or mow the grass while the family is away on vacation? These few suggestions will trigger your imagination to think of others that may better fit your lifestyle and schedule.

Appeal to people at their point of felt need

There is still one more consideration under the heading of preevangelism. We must overcome natural barriers; we must see the potential in the individual; we must build bridges of friendship. We must also appeal to the other person at his or her point of felt need.

Everyone has a hunger or a thirst for something. We call this a felt need. And any effective spiritual outreach should begin with an effort to discover and meet that need. If you want to build a church, someone has well said, find a need and meet it, find a hurt and heal it. Jesus reached out to the Samaritan woman at her point of need:

> If you knew the gift of God and who it is that asks you for a drink, you would have asked him and he would have given you living water. (4:10)

The woman had a deep inner thirst that the water she carried day after day from the well to her home could not satisfy. Now at last she was face to face with a Man who offered her water to quench the deep, deep thirst of her inner soul.

Denise and her evangelism team knocked on an apartment door in West Omaha. They were greeted by Al, a contractor from Chicago who was building a local theater. Al invited the group into the dining room. First, Al wanted to show them his new solitaire card game. The team watched as he explained it. Then they listened as the man described in great detail his background. Everything he said spoke loudly of his desperate loneliness. But before the team could present the gospel to Al, it was time to go.

"Aren't you going to give me some of your literature?" Al asked Denise as the team rose to leave. "Aren't you going to invite me to your church?" They gave Al some literature and invited him to the early Sunday morning church service.

Denise called Carol, whom she knew would be a greeter at the early service. She described Al and asked Carol to keep an eye out for him.

"Don't laugh, Al"

Meanwhile, Al spent an evening at a nearby bar. In the course of conversation he told the other fellows there about his three visitors. He laughed as he mentioned their invitation to him to attend Christ Community Church.

"Don't laugh, Al," they countered. "Have you ever driven on the interstate past that church on Sunday morning? They must have something going for them, judging from all the cars in their parking lot."

Intrigued by the comments at the bar, early Sunday morning Al headed for Christ Community Church just off the interstate. As he walked in the front door, Carol met him with a bright smile.

"You must be Al!" Carol said.

"How did you know *me*?" Al wanted to know.

"Denise said you would be coming this morning. It's great to have you here!"

Desiring to be unnoticed, Al slipped into a back pew. The woman next to him gave him a warm greeting. An usher had a welcome packet for him. The singing and special music expressed a warmth and joy he had never experienced before. And at the end of Pastor Bob's message, Al prayed silently, inviting Christ into his life.

After the worship service, someone led Al to a Sunday school class. It was Denise's. When Denise introduced Al, everyone in the class reached out to him in love and acceptance. Al found his need for love and fellowship being met in a most unexpected way. He returned Wednesday evening for the prayer meeting. He wanted to know if there were other activities at the church that he could attend.

If we are serious about disciple-making, pre-evangelism is a must. We need to learn from and follow the example of the Master Discipler.

2. Presentation

In chapter 8, I emphasized from Paul's second letter to Timothy the importance of formulating the gospel, learning a gospel presentation, equipping people to give an answer for the hope within them and multiplying our witness through the training of others. In this chapter I want you, in John 4, to watch Jesus Himself make a gospel presentation to the Samaritan woman at the well near Sychar.

While ministering to a missionary conference in Japan, I was invited to have lunch with a group of Japanese pastors, all of whom had studied Evangelism Explosion. There was a feeling among them that the E.E. presentation was too American for effective use in Japan.

After some small talk, we got to the point. "What is it in E.E. that you feel will not work in Japan?" I asked.

One of the pastors spoke up. "One serious problem," he said, "is for the outline to begin with the statement that heaven is a free gift." In Japanese culture, such a start seemed too abrupt. They preferred first to speak of God and later to come around to God's free gift of eternal life.

"Was Jesus American or Asian?" I countered.

"Asian!" On that point there was consensus.

"If that is so, and if I can convince you that Jesus used the basic E.E. outline in witnessing to Asians, would that help?"

"Of course!" they agreed.

I asked the pastors to turn to John 3. I showed them, point by point, that Jesus in his witness to Nicodemus used all five main points of the E.E. gospel presentation: grace (heaven is a free gift), man, God, Christ, faith.

"But Nicodemus wasn't a typical Asian," the

pastors objected. "His background was Jewish. He knew the Old Testament. Jesus could use such an outline with him."

"Well," I went on, "let's turn to the next chapter—John 4. What about the Samaritan woman? Did she have an Old Testament background?"

They agreed that the Samaritan woman probably knew little about the Jewish Scriptures.

Then I began to show them that Jesus covered not only all five points of the E.E. outline with the Samaritan woman, but He covered them *in the exact E.E. sequence.*

Grace—heaven is a free gift

Jesus said to the Samaritan woman at the well,

> If you knew the gift of God, . . . you would have asked . . . and he would have given you living water. . . . The water I give . . . will become . . . a spring of water welling up to eternal life. (4:10, 14)

When the woman responded by requesting this water of eternal life (1:15), Jesus went on to the second point of the outline.

Man—a sinner and sinful

Jesus approached the delicate subject of sin very carefully.

> Go, call your husband and come back. (4:16)

When the woman said she had no husband, Jesus concurred, pointing out that the man she was presently living with was not her husband. In other words, Jesus was calling her attention to the sin that needed to be dealt with.

The woman, uncomfortable, promptly changed the subject. She asked about the proper place of worship. Was it on sacred Mount Gerizim in Samaria or was it on Mount Moriah in Jerusalem? Jesus answered her question, but He returned immediately to the gospel, introducing the third point in His presentation.

God—both Father and Spirit

Jesus said to the Samaritan woman,

> A time is coming and has now come when the true worshipers will worship the Father in spirit and truth, for they are the kind of worshipers the Father seeks. God is spirit, and his worshipers must worship in spirit and in truth. (4:23–24)

Jesus' statement about worship and God led the woman to bring up the subject of the promised Messiah (4:25). When Jesus made His claim, "I who speak to you am he" (4:26), the Samaritan was at the fourth point of the gospel.

Christ

Notice how gradually the woman came to an understanding of who Jesus was. He was a Jew (4:9), someone greater than Jacob (4:12–14), a Prophet (4:19), the Christ (4:29), the Savior of the world (4:22). Not only did the woman come to an understanding of who Jesus is, but she also learned why He came. He came to bring salvation to the world.

Faith

This revelation so excited the Samaritan woman that she put her faith in Jesus, receiving His gift of eternal life.

> Leaving her water jar, the woman went back to the town and said to the people, "Come, see a man who told me everything I ever did. Could this be the Christ?" (4:28–29)

I do not take her question to her townspeople to indicate any doubt on her part, but rather to lead her people gently into the same glorious revelation she had received. In fact, the woman's faith was so strong that it seems to have ignited faith in a number of other people:

> Many of the Samaritans from that town believed in him because of the woman's testimony. (4:39)

When my Japanese pastor friends saw that the E.E. outline had such biblical precedent, they agreed that it should be used unchanged in Japan—even as it has been used in scores of other countries around the world.

In sharing this incident, I am not suggesting

that the E.E. outline is the only adequate presentation. There are other approaches equally as biblical. I share it simply to point out that the E.E. outline is biblical and therefore usable anywhere.

3. Priorities

A priority is a "condition of precedence in time, order or importance." Once the Samaritan woman had come to faith in Christ, what was the priority item on her agenda? Was it not to witness to her family, friends and townspeople? Was it not to become, herself, a reproducing disciple?

> Leaving her water jar, the woman went back to the town and said to the people, "Come see a man who told me everything I ever did. Could this be the Christ?" They came out of the town and made their way toward him. . . .
> Many of the Samaritans from that town believed in him because of the woman's testimony. (4:28–30, 39)

Archie Parrish, founder and president of Serve International, had an experience similar to that of the Samaritan woman. The man who led him to Christ put reproducing high on Archie's priority list. In fact, the very next day he took Archie with him to witness to another person, and the next day to someone else. And the following day and every day thereafter for weeks he gave Archie on-the-job training in personal evangelism. It was several months before Archie discovered that all Christians were not out doing the same thing. He assumed every other believer from new birth was, like him, reproducing!

Fred and his wife, Peggy, are examples from our church of new Christians who went to work at once. Shortly after Fred and Peggy came to Christ, they enrolled in our Evangelism Explosion training. They grew rapidly in the Word, in prayer and in leading a number of their family to Christ. They were baptized on the Sunday evening of an Evangelism Explosion leadership training clinic for pastors, missionaries and lay leaders.

The next three evenings, Fred and Peggy surprised the participants in the clinic by serving as trainers and taking them out into the community for on-the-job training in evangelism. Before long, they themselves were trained in a clinic and began teaching evangelism and training disciples in our church's daughter congregations in and around Omaha. Fred became an elder of our church, was elected to serve as president of our Alliance Men organization and started the lay pastoral training program of our church district. Today Fred is serving as outreach pastor of a dynamic and growing Alliance church. He is reproducing over and over through the many people he has trained.

Different priorities

God's kingdom first. That has been Fred and Peggy's priority. It was Jesus' priority as he dealt with the Samaritan woman. By contrast, note how out of touch Jesus' 12 disciples were with His kingdom interests:

> Just then his disciples returned and were surprised to find him talking with a woman. . . .
>
> His disciples urged him, "Rabbi, eat something." . . .
>
> "My food," said Jesus, "is to do the will of him who sent me and to finish his work. Do you not say, 'Four months more and then the harvest'? I tell you, open your eyes and look at the fields! They are ripe for harvest." (4:27, 31, 34–35)

The disciples were primarily concerned about their physical needs. But Jesus placed the spiritual needs of the woman at the top of His agenda. The disciples went to the town in search of bread. The newly converted woman set down her water jar and ran to the town in search of lost men and women!

What are your priorities in life? Are you caught up in the search for "bread"? Or are you doing the will of Him who saved you and left you in this world to finish His work? Do you really realize you were born to reproduce?

A Christian welder, Wayne, spent 50 years of his life with an unbiblical agenda. When his wife died of cancer, he grew bitter and quit going to church. But then a friend invited him to drive almost an hour to our church in Omaha. In Christ Community Church Wayne found comfort, strength and new purpose in life. He learned to share his faith. Equipped in evangelism, he became very fruitful in leading people to Christ.

Then Wayne discovered the joy of training others to be evangelists. When I needed someone to travel with me to assist in clinics I was holding for pastors, Wayne volunteered. Between trips to Georgia, New York, Minnesota, Washington, D.C., the Philippines, Nigeria, Ghana and the West Indies, Wayne welds "to pay expenses." What an example he has become of a reproducing disciple! He has discovered Christ's priorities and lives by them.

You were born to reproduce

Jesus' last command—I say it again—was to "go and make disciples of all nations." How does that fit into your order of priorities? You were born to reproduce. And the people God has used you to win to Him were also born to be fruitful and multiply.

How are you doing?

How are your disciples doing?

Study Questions

John 4

1. Do you think that the Samaritan woman at the well initially looked like a good prospect for personal evangelism? Why?

2. What was she really saying in her response to Jesus' request for a drink? To His statement about the gift of God and the water of life?

3. What are some of the cultural barriers that you face as you seek to witness to Christ today? How can they be overcome?

4. How do you respond to the statement: "Before we can win people to Christ, we must win them to ourselves"? Explain how you deal with this matter.

5. How soon after a person trusts Christ as Savior should we begin training that person to share his or her faith? Why? How?

CHAPTER 10

Encountering Seeking People

Acts 8

I HAVE JUST HAD THE THRILL OF encountering two seeking people—Jim and his wife Ali. Both were born into religious homes; neither had pursued with any zest the parental faith. But having moved into a new home and a new community and looking forward to a new family member, they decided they needed a new faith.

In their search for God they had visited several churches. When I met them they were ripened fruit ready to fall at the slightest touch of an outstretched hand. Both of them received Christ with the faith of a little child. It was marvelous to see!

Such encounters remind me again that all around us are more people searching for Jesus

Christ than there are evangelists in our churches equipped and willing to go out and help them find Him.

God has committed Himself to respond to the person who seeks Him seriously. That is the story of the Ethiopian official told in Acts 8.

> Now an angel of the Lord said to Philip, "Go south to the road—the desert road—that goes down from Jerusalem to Gaza." So he started out, and on his way he met an Ethiopian eunuch, an important official in charge of all the treasury of Candace, queen of the Ethiopians. This man had gone to Jerusalem to worship, and on his way home was sitting in his chariot reading the book of Isaiah the prophet. (8:26–28)

How do we know that the Ethiopian was seeking God? First, this man busy in the treasury of his queen had taken time to travel the great distance from Ethiopia to Jerusalem to worship God. Second, he searched for God in the Hebrew Scriptures—and, of all the books, in Isaiah. Third, he evidenced great eagerness, not waiting until he arrived home, but reading from his cumbersome scroll in a bumpy chariot.

Whom did God send to take the gospel to this seeking man? He sent a Spirit-filled lay person (Acts 6:3, 5) already very active in evangelism

(8:5–6, 12). And God used this lay person, Philip, in a very beautiful way to lead the Ethiopian official to Christ. It is a biblical example from which we can learn 11 practical steps as we encounter seeking people.

Step 1. Get Started

The Scripture text puts it very simply: "So [Philip] started out." Both the Vietnamese and the Chinese have a common saying. "In 10,000 tasks, getting started is the most difficult." That is true in every culture! Whether it is homework, letter writing, dish washing, house cleaning, piano practicing, jogging, lighting a charcoal fire or mowing the lawn, the most difficult step is getting started.

Witnessing is no different. Overcoming the physical and spiritual inertia that "glues" us to our comfortable Lazy Boy chairs is not easy. When the Holy Spirit prompts us to go to someone with the good news, a thousand good but lower priority items crowd in to capture our attention. We are distracted by a multitude of excuses:

> *I don't have time.*
> *He's not really interested.*
> *No one will be home.*
> *People don't like to talk about "religion."*
> *This just isn't the most convenient time.*
> *Witnessing is not my forte.*

Sometimes we do not witness because we are afraid of making mistakes. But the worst mistake of all is not getting started! Of course you will make some mistakes! I did. Everyone does. But if you are prompted by faith, obedience, love and humility, God the Holy Spirit will use you and accomplish His purposes in spite of your mistakes.

When in Hong Kong I first attempted to share my faith using the Evangelism Explosion method, I made every possible mistake. In visiting Joyce, the Cathay Pacific flight attendant who had been to our church, I took two other men with me; one person should have been a woman. I had not yet committed the gospel outline to memory; I should have. I took a large, conspicuous Bible, not a small New Testament. But God's Spirit worked in spite of my blunders. Joyce received Christ as her Savior.

Only the moving ship can be steered. Once we get moving, God will steer us to people ripe for the gospel—people like the Ethiopian official, people like Joyce.

2. Get Near

Philip, the Spirit-filled deacon-evangelist, had been in the midst of a busy ministry in Samaria before God steered him to a lone chariot en route from Jerusalem to Gaza. Once in sight of the chariot bearing the Ethiopian financial officer, Philip received further instructions.

> The Spirit told Philip, "Go to that chariot and stay near it." (8:29)

Nowhere in the Bible are sinners told to go to church. But saints are told to go to sinners. In His prayer to God on behalf of His disciples, Jesus said, "As you sent me into the world, I have sent them into the world" (John 17:18).

We smile at the nursery rhyme about Simple Simon sitting in his backyard fishing from a barrel. To catch fish a person has to be where the fish are. But ministers continue to preach their best evangelistic sermons to congregations of born-again Christians.

Jesus ate with sinners, asked them for a drink of water, visited in their homes, paused to meet their needs as He walked from town to town. If we are going to impact the world for Christ, we too must make contact with the people who need Him. We must build bridges to them where they are: in the workplace, the marketplace, the beauty parlor, the tennis club, the classroom, the neighborhood.

Psychologically near, too

Not only do we need to "draw near to" the sinners in a geographic sense, but we need to draw near them psychologically. Saints and sinners are oftentimes on totally different wavelengths. Saints may be meditating on heavenly matters or church activities; sinners may be wrestling with such earthly issues as putting food on the table or saving a crumbling marriage.

Jesus drew near to people by building psychological bridges. He talked about the things within their everyday experiences— sheep, flowers, bread, wind, mountains. Then He moved gradually to heavenly truths.

Paul declared, "I have become all things to all men so that by all possible means I might save some" (1 Corinthians 9:22).

One day in Vietnam, I was walking with Pastor Doan Van Mieng through a village. We were looking for an opportunity to introduce someone to Christ Jesus. Spotting an elderly man watering flowers in his front yard, we paused to give him a gospel tract and to share our witness. But we were met by total indifference. We wished the man a good day and started down the path to look for someone more responsive.

But suddenly Pastor Mieng stopped and then turned back to ask the man some questions about his flowers. What were the names of the various plants? What kind of fertilizers did he use? What was his secret for growing such a lush garden? The man immediately softened, inviting us into his home for a cup of tea. After we had further discussed his flowers—his pride-and-joy—he began to ask questions about the gospel.

On another occasion I was on a similar village visit with Pastor Nguyen Van Thin. Both of us were dressed in lightweight suits with ties—the customary attire of the clergy in Vietnam. But our dress was not very appropriate for conversation with shirtless, sweaty, sawdust-covered carpenters. I wondered how we might identify with them. My pastor friend provided the answer.

"Say, this is a very strong and attractive house you're building," he called out. "What kind of wood are you using?"

"This is mahogany," one of the men replied. "White ants will never touch it!"

As Pastor Thin asked more questions, the men set aside their saws, climbed down their ladders and donned their shirts.

"We're in construction, too," said the pastor. "We're involved in building houses in heaven—houses not made of wood or thatch but of gold, silver and precious stones."

Pastor Thin had captured their attention. From that point he went on to share the wonderful news of Jesus Christ and His love. He had demonstrated the importance of drawing near geographically and psychologically. Having captured the attention of these carpenters and won their friendship, he could share with them the wonderful news of eternal life.

3. Grasp Opportunities

Philip did not let any grass grow under his feet! The Scriptures go on to inform us,

Then Philip ran up to the chariot. (8:30)

Had Philip paused to consider whether or not to proceed, the chariot might have been out of reach. Philip would have missed his chance to witness.

When God puts similar opportunity before us, we must not hesitate, speculate, vacillate, procrastinate or even delegate! We must *run!* Cervantes, the Spanish writer, said, "Delay always breeds danger, and to postpone a great design is often to ruin it." Someone else advised, "Defer not until tomorrow to be wise; tomorrow's sun to thee may never rise." Another has quipped, "One of these days really means *none* of these days."

The element of time is crucial! Ripe fruit, left unpicked too long, rots. A whitened harvest, if neglected, becomes a financial disaster. In the spiritual realm, lost opportunities mean eternally lost people—and blood on our hands (Ezekiel 33:8).

One of my deepest regrets arises from such a missed opportunity. For a number of years I prayed for a couple who lived next door to us in Omaha. Donna and I extended love and friendship to them. We watched for the right opening to share the gospel. Then we discovered they were moving away. As they were packing up, I walked over to see what I could do to help. My neighbor spied the two-question-mark pin on my lapel and asked what it meant. I knew my neighbor was busy. It did not seem like a good time to involve her in a gospel presentation.

"Oh, the pin is an award that we are given when we complete an evangelism class at church," I explained, totally evading the chief purpose of the pin. I thereby missed the occasion for which I had been praying. Not likely will I ever have another opportunity to share with her.

In Mechanicsburg, Pennsylvania, some time later, while greeting worshipers after a service at which I had preached, I was approached by two young men in their 20s. One of the two, as he shook my hand, spied my lapel pin.

"Pastor," he wanted to know, "what do the two question marks stand for?"

"Those? They are two questions that were asked of every presidential candidate in the recent election. They are two of the most important questions that have ever been asked. In fact, they are questions that have totally changed hundreds of people's lives." I could tell by the look on his face that Joe was really curious (I learned his name was Joe).

"Joe," I continued, "I never tell anyone what

the questions are unless the person promises to give me his answer."

"OK," Joe agreed. "I promise! What are they?"

"The first is—and I hope you live to be a hundred, but—*if* you were to die today, do you know for certain that you'd go to be with God in heaven?"

"I hope so," Joe responded. "Can anyone know that for sure?"

"Joe, *I* know, and thousands—millions—of other people know."

I pulled my little New Testament from my pocket. "This little book tells how you can know that for sure. But let me ask you the second question: If you were to die today, and God were to say to you, 'Joe, why should I let you into My heaven?' what would you answer?"

"Well, let's see—I guess I'd say, 'I'm not on drugs. I live a clean life.' "

"Joe, you're to be commended!" I responded. "In this day and age there aren't that many fellows who can say that. You know, when you answered my first question, I said to myself, *I've got something really great to share with Joe.* But now that I've heard your answer to the second question, I know I have something fabulous to tell you. Are you in a hurry to go somewhere, or would you have a few minutes for us to visit together?"

Joe was anxious to hear more. He and his

friend, who had been praying for Joe for a whole year and who had brought him to church that morning, went with me into the pastor's study. A half hour later Joe gave his heart to Christ.

How important it is to be alert and prepared for the opportunities God brings our way!

4. Listen Carefully

All effective evangelism begins with listening. It was so as Philip met the Ethiopian officer.

> Philip ran up to the chariot and heard the man. (8:30)

One major advantage of personal evangelism over pulpit or crusade evangelism is the opportunity to listen and discover where the sinner really is. Only as we know where the person is coming from can we tailor our presentation to meet his or her specific needs. By listening we also are letting the person know we are interested in him or her. We build a friendship and thus earn the right to share the gospel.

Listening is not simply waiting our turn to speak or pausing while we think of what to say next. It is giving our undivided attention, it is looking the person in the eye, it is responding physically to what the other is saying by a nod, a smile, an expression of pain. It may be repeating phrases the other person has said. When we are truly listening, we will not look away or look at our watches. We will avoid yawning, frowning, slouching or interrupting.

Could it be that God gave us two ears and one mouth because He wants us to listen twice as much as we speak?

The importance of listening was unforgettably impressed on me while visiting a distinguished elderly Chinese gentleman in Hong Kong. When I asked him if he was sure he was going to heaven, he spent the rest of the evening answering my question. I listened in rapt attention. The man invited me back for a second visit to continue our discussion.

When I asked him what he would say to God at heaven's gate, he again spent the whole evening answering my question. When our visit ended, he told me he had found the conversation so interesting that he wanted to invite me to dinner at the Jockey Club to talk more with him. At last, on that third encounter, I had earned the right to share the gospel with him. He listened attentively to what I had to say and responded enthusiastically.

Solomon wrote, "He who answers before listening—/ that is his folly and his shame" (Proverbs 18:13).

The wise personal evangelist will cultivate the lost art of listening and thus prepare the way for witnessing.

5. Ask Questions

Asking questions is another art that an effective witness must develop. Philip had a question for the man in the chariot reading Isaiah the prophet.

> "Do you understand what you are reading?" Philip asked.
> "How can I," [the Ethiopian] said, "unless someone explains it to me?" (8:30–31)

Not just any questions will do. They must be the kinds of questions that move a person from discussing the peripheral areas of life to the deeper core of existence. These questions need to penetrate the heart of the person and his or her situation. One of the greatest errors made in witnessing is the failure to ask exploratory questions that uncover the other person's background, spiritual condition and felt needs. A person unable to ask good questions will make incorrect assessments and take wrong actions.

In E.E., we train people to begin by asking questions about the other person's secular life: "How many children does he have? How long has she lived here? What does he do for a living? What does she do for relaxation?" We call these surface questions, the who-what-where-when-how questions. The witness may want then to ask some why questions that move into the deeper realm of motives: "Why did you move to Omaha?" "How did you happen to take up medicine?"

Next, we suggest asking questions about the person's religious background: "How often do you go to church?" "How long have you followed this particular faith?" Or, if the person has made a religious change, "What prompted you to make this change?" If it is a person who has visited our church, we may ask, "What were your impressions of our church?" (We avoid asking their impressions of the sermon lest the discussion get side-tracked on something other than the gospel.)

Finally, we ask the deeper questions about eternal life—the questions I asked Joe after the church service in Pennsylvania.

6. Obtain Permission

Before we ask any of the serious questions, we are careful always to seek the other person's permission. Philip did not force himself and his religious views upon the African. He waited for an invitation.

> So [the Ethiopian] invited Philip to come up and sit with him. (8:31)

A person's home, a person's life and a person's religious faith are the three areas generally most carefully guarded by people.

No one should intrude into any of these sacrosanct domains without express permission. Just as we would not enter a person's home without permission, so we should not invade the privacy of a person's life or religion without permission. Yet, too frequently, we attempt to do so by our gospel witness. *Always first obtain permission.*

In our E.E. classes, we train the personal evangelists to preface their diagnostic questions about eternal life with a simple, "May I ask you a question?" It is amazing what a difference it makes! We also train them to ask before sharing the gospel, "May I share with you how I discovered eternal life and how you can know it, too?" If they cannot secure an affirmative response, they should not proceed.

One of my trainees, Nick, asked me to pray for a Saturday afternoon boat ride he was going to take with his uncle, a university professor. Nick asked me to pray that he might be able to share the gospel with his uncle. When Nick arrived in class the following week, I asked how things had gone.

"My uncle almost threw me in the bay!" Nick complained.

"Let me ask one question, Nick," I responded. "Did you ask your uncle's permission to share the gospel with him?"

Nick seemed surprised. "Is that important?" he queried.

"Important? It's absolutely critical—as you

can now see in retrospect. You invaded a private area of your uncle's life without his permission." It was an unintentional blunder, but it was serious.

7. Use Scripture

Once we have permission to present the gospel, we must take another cue from Philip. He used the Scriptures.

> Then Philip began with that very passage of Scripture and told him the good news. (8:35)

Life comes from a seed. Light comes from a lamp. God's Word is both the Seed that gives life and the Lamp that gives light. Paul wrote Timothy, "The holy Scriptures . . . are able to make you wise for salvation through faith in Christ Jesus" (2 Timothy 3:15). He said to the Roman Christians, "Faith comes from hearing the message, and the message is heard through the Word of Christ" (Romans 10:17). John, referring to his own inspired letter as God's Word, said, "I write these things to you who believe in the name of the Son of God so that you may know that you have eternal life" (1 John 5:13). It may be helpful at times to refer to philosophy, science, logic or current events. Anecdote and illustration may clarify truth.

But it is the Word of God that brings conviction, faith, light and life.

Even one verse of God's Word has enough power to transform the worst of sinners. A woman whose husband was an alcoholic led a most miserable life until someone gave her a Bible and she was converted to Christ Jesus. She found comfort in reading the Scriptures, and the Bible became her most treasured possession.

A sobering discovery

The woman's husband sneered at her newfound religion. One day, when he came home half-intoxicated, he snatched the book from her and threw it into the fireplace.

"Now we'll see what will be left of your precious Bible!"

The next morning as he was cleaning out the ashes, he noticed a few pages of his wife's Bible had not burned. His eyes fell upon Jesus' words in Matthew 24:35: "Heaven and earth will pass away, but my words will never pass away." Startled and sobered, the man found himself convicted by the Holy Spirit. Soon the same Holy Spirit brought saving faith to him.

If we want to be effective witnesses for Jesus Christ, we must commit to memory key verses of Scripture that we may use in leading people to faith in Christ. We will also be advised to carry in our pocket or purse a small New Testament that we can use to turn to Scriptures not yet memorized.

When I witness to Roman Catholics, I often ask them if they have a copy of the Scriptures, and I use their Bibles. (Philip used the Ethiopian's scroll to tell him the good news about Jesus.) Frequently they are amazed to discover that the saving truth I am sharing with them is right in their own Bibles.

8. Proclaim Christ

Using the Scriptures when we witness is important. But their purpose in our witness is to proclaim Christ.

> Philip began with that very passage of Scripture and told [the Ethiopian] the good news about Jesus. (8:35)

Christianity is not a religion but a relationship—with Jesus Christ. When Philip made use of the Ethiopian's scroll, his focus was on Jesus. Jesus Christ is central in the Scriptures. He is central in our witness. He is the One who saves us from the penalty of our sins and gives us eternal life. Jesus is our Message!

The Samaritan woman said, "Come, see a man who told me everything I ever did. Could this be the Christ?" (John 4:29). John the Baptist's message was unmistakably clear: "Look, the Lamb of God, who takes away the

sin of the world!" (John 1:29). Peter proclaimed
Christ to the rulers, elders and teachers of the
law meeting in Jerusalem with the high priest:
"Salvation is found in no one else, for there is
no other name under heaven given to men by
which we must be saved" (Acts 4:12).

Paul testified to the Corinthians about his
witness: "When I came to you, brothers, I did
not come with eloquence or superior wisdom
as I proclaimed to you the testimony about
God. For I resolved to know nothing while I
was with you except Jesus Christ and him
crucified" (1 Corinthians 2:1–2). And when
asked the way to heaven, Jesus Christ
responded unmistakably clearly: "I am the way
and the truth and the life. No one comes to the
Father except through me" (John 14:6).

The message of the entire Bible is Jesus
Christ. A.W. Tozer, writing in *Renewed Day by
Day* says,

> I do not mind telling you that I have al-
> ways found Jesus Christ beckoning to me
> throughout the Scriptures. I am convinced
> that it was God's design that we should
> find the divine Creator, Redeemer and
> Lord whenever and wherever we search
> the Scriptures . . . Our Lord Jesus Christ
> was that One divinely commissioned to set
> forth the mystery and the majesty and the
> wonder and the glory of the Godhead
> throughout the universe. It is more than an

accident that both the Old and New Testaments comb heaven and earth for figures of speech or simile to set forth the wonder and glory of God!

9. Expect Decisions

Having prolaimed Christ by properly using the Scriptures, we should expect a positive decision. Philip seemed unsurprised at the Ethiopian's positive response to his gospel presentation. Having been sent by the Holy Spirit on this specific assignment, Philip expected success.

> The eunuch said, "Look, here is water. Why shouldn't I be baptized?" (8:36)

A fisherman always pulls in his line or net. A farmer "puts in the sickle" at harvesttime. A salesman endeavors to close the sale. So the personal evangelist must expect—and ask for—a decision.

I mentioned earlier that the word *decision* is in the name of one of the best known evangelical radio and TV programs and in the name of a widely distributed evangelical magazine. It was no accident that Billy Graham, the foremost evangelist of our day, should name his magazine *Decision* or call his television and radio programs "The Hour of Decision." Billy

Graham expects decisions! And God blesses his ministry with thousands.

But simply to expect decisions for Christ is inadequate. We must take steps to assure ourselves of those decisions. We must know exactly what we are going to say and how we are going to say it. In E.E. we urge our trainees to memorize carefully and use consistently a step by step procedure for bringing people to a solid, biblical commitment. If you are serious about winning family, friends and associates to Christ, you will do well to obtain this material and learn it.

A very critical step

This Step 9 in the witnessing encounter is critical. It is so eternally important that we urge our trainees to over-learn it. That is because if anything is going to go wrong in our gospel presentation, it will go wrong here! The telephone will ring, the coffee will spill, the baby will wake up and begin crying, the Great Dane will decide to become a lap dog, an unexpected visitor will drop by. Satan will use every imaginable distraction to keep the person to whom we are witnessing from a commitment to Christ. And if we are not well prepared and ready for such distractions, we will not be able to nail down the commitment.

Paul says a proper commitment involves two very important parts of a person: heart and mouth. "It is with your heart that you believe and are justified, and it is with your mouth that you confess and are saved" (Romans 10:10).

The Ethiopian made such a commitment. In asking for baptism, he was clearly signifying that he had put his faith in Jesus Christ. Philip understood the man's request in that light.

10. Follow Up

That brings us to another very important step: follow up.

> [The African official] gave orders to stop the chariot. Then both Philip and the eunuch went down into the water and Philip baptized him. (8:38)

When someone comes to faith in Christ, it is absolutely essential that he or she be carefully followed up and rooted in the church. As with Philip, the primary responsibility for nurture and growth rests upon the person leading the other one to Christ.

When Bob led Doug and Lori to Christ, he took very seriously this biblical principle. Every Sunday for several months he accompanied them to the New Believers Sunday school class. He sat with them in church. He and his wife, Sue, invited them home for Sunday dinner. Every week Bob and Sue brought them to a discipleship class where they learned to pray and apply God's Word to their lives.

It was no surprise then that Doug and Lori grew rapidly in Christ and soon became pillars in the church. But the day came when they moved away from Omaha. What would happen now? What could the Omaha church do about them at this point?

11. Trust God

It was important at that juncture that the church entrust Doug and Lori to God. Philip had to do so with the Ethiopian official.

> When they came up out of the water, the Spirit of the Lord suddenly took Philip away, and the eunuch did not see him again, but went on his way rejoicing. (8:39)

It is significant that God initiated this encounter by directing Philip to "Go" (8:29). And when Philip's ministry was complete, "the Spirit of the Lord suddenly took Philip away" (8:39). Philip was a Spirit-filled (6:3), Spirit-led (8:39) deacon. His witness and his follow-up were not the result of human ingenuity, clever reasoning or psychological manipulation. They were done in total dependence upon the Spirit of God.

What would happen to the Ethiopian financial officer when Philip was taken away? What would happen when he himself had to return alone to Ethiopia? I am thankful that the Holy

Spirit went with him, enabling him to stand true to Christ and to grow strong in the Lord. Although the book of Acts does not record for us what happened to the new believer once he was back in Ethiopia, he must have witnessed widely. How do I know that? Ben, a member of our church from Ethiopia, tells me that today there is in his homeland a church that traces its roots back to this man whom Philip led to Christ 20 centuries ago on the road home from Jerusalem.

God is faithful! If we will trust Him in the 11 steps of our witness to, and discipleship of, those we lead to Christ, God will do His part in keeping these new believers true to Himself. God will build them up until they attain to the whole measure of the fullness of Christ.

Will you do your part?

If not you, who? If not now, when?

Discover the area of greatest need

As you do your part, will you take Christ's saving message not only to respected, rich, upper-class, religiously-inclined people, but to the down-and-outers, the wounded, the bruised, the bleeding, the ones abandoned by society and neglected by the church—and to those in between?

In the three remaining chapters you will discover one of today's most needy, yet neglected, fields for evangelism. And if you are concerned about your neighbors, turn immediately to the next chapter and ask God to speak to you about how you can be used to rescue some truly hurting people around you.

Study Questions

Acts 8

1. Why does the Ethiopian eunuch visit Jerusalem and what does that tell us about his spiritual condition?
2. If he was already a worshiper of the true God and was reading his Bible, why was it urgent that God should send Philip to witness to him?
3. What is the relationship between God's preparation and Philip's initiative in this narrative?
4. How might you better prepare yourself for similar opportunities?
5. Are you witnessing regularly for Christ or is there something keeping you from getting started? If you are not witnessing, how might you overcome such spiritual inertia?
6. Think back over your past two to three years and describe one or two witnessing opportunities God has brought your way. How did you handle the situation? How might you have improved your approach?
7. Why do you think it is important to ask permission before sharing the gospel? What difference does it make?

8. Why is it important to use Scripture in witnessing? What are your five favorite Scriptures to use in witnessing?

9. How do you account for Philip's weak follow-up of the Ethiopian? What would you have done if you had a similar situation on an airplane?

CHAPTER 11

Rescuing Hurting Strangers

Luke 10

OUR WORLD IS NO FRIEND to strangers. The only friend a stranger can find may be another stranger. And that is only because both persons suffer from a common pain called loneliness.

A generation ago the primitive Aucas of Ecuador killed Phil Saint, Jim Elliot and three other missionaries who were attempting to contact them with the gospel. The reason: they were strangers.

The Chinese of Hong Kong call non-Chinese from other lands "foreign devils." Even in our own country, which prides itself on its civility, immigrants frequently receive harsh treatment from people who themselves have never been strangers in a foreign country.

I heard about two salesmen—New Yorkers—waiting for a commuter train to take them into the city. A stranger approached one of the men to ask for the time. The salesman totally ignored him. He asked again, and again was ignored.

"Why did you act that way?" the other salesman asked after the stranger had walked away. "You have a watch, don't you?"

"Listen," explained the first salesman. "I'm standing here minding my own business. This guy wants to know what time it is. So maybe I tell him. We get talking and the guy says, 'How about a drink?' So we have a drink, and then we have more drinks. Finally I say, 'Come on out to my house for a bite to eat.' And at my house we're eating sandwiches when my 21-year-old daughter comes in. So she falls in love with this guy, and he falls for her. Then they get married, and I have in my family a guy who can't afford a watch! No, I don't want him in my family."

The yarn may be far-fetched, but it underscores the problem. People are reluctant to become involved with strangers. Involvement might cost them something. It could be an inconvenience. It would take some of their precious time.

Another focus

Until now in this book we have thought together primarily of friendship evangelism—

that is, of introducing Christ to family, friends, associates. But there is another group of people all around us. They are the strangers, and often they are lonely and hurting.

In His story of the Good Samaritan, recorded in Luke 10:25–37, Jesus addresses in an unforgettable way this subject of strangers who are hurting. We will take a minute to look at the context of the story and then at the story itself.

In the course of Jesus' ministry—we are not told exactly where, but it likely was in or near Jerusalem, judging by the details of Jesus' story—a young lawyer stood to his feet with a question.

> "Teacher," he asked, "what must I do to inherit eternal life?" (10:25)

The question asked by the young lawyer was the most important question anyone could possibly ask. But Luke says the lawyer posed the question to test Jesus. He may not have been sincere. And by the way he worded his question—"What must I *do?*"—the lawyer seems to have felt he had to *earn* eternal life.

Jesus did not reply directly. He responded with a counter question.

> "What is written in the Law?" [Jesus] replied. "How do you read it?" (10:26)

In other words, Jesus was saying, "You're a

lawyer. What does the Law say?" The young lawyer replied that the Law of Moses required perfect love toward God and neighbor.

> "You have answered correctly," Jesus replied. "Do this and you will live." (10:28)

"Who is my neighbor?"

But the lawyer knew only too well that he had not loved God and neighbor perfectly—and could not. Looking for a way to salve his guilty conscience, he asked Jesus a second question:

> And who is my neighbor? (10:29)

Referring again to Vine's *Dictionary of New Testament Words*, we learn that the Greek word for *neighbor* encompassed much more than does our English word, which refers to someone living nearby. It included everyone in a given community whom a person might encounter, including strangers with whom the person might deal.

In answering the lawyer's question, Jesus tells a story about some travelers on the road between Jerusalem and Jericho. All four apparently walked the road rather frequently.

I personally made the trip from Jerusalem to Jericho, not on foot but in a Mercedes touring car. The road, 17 miles long, runs northeast from Jerusalem down a steep, 3,000-foot descent. The country, now as then, is desolate and wild. There are numerous places that could serve as hideouts for robbers bent on attacking unsuspecting travelers.

In His story, Jesus speaks of four kinds of travelers on the road from Jerusalem to Jericho. We will look at all four.

1. Criminal

A man was going down from Jerusalem to Jericho, when he fell into the hands of robbers. They stripped him of his clothes, beat him and went away, leaving him half dead. (10:30)

The road from Jerusalem to Jericho, with its craggy rocks and sudden turns was notoriously dangerous. In his commentary on the Gospel of Luke, William Barclay says the road by the fifth century had seen so many killings that it was dubbed the "bloody way." In the 19th century, travelers, to be assured of a safe trip, had to pay off local robber bands. Even so, Englishman Sir Frederick Henniker was stripped and killed. And as late as 1930, H.V. Morton was warned to get home before dark because of Abu Jildah's adeptness at holding up cars, robbing travelers and escaping into the hills before police could arrive.

Criminals are not confined to the road between Jerusalem and Jericho. In the urban centers of America, and even in smaller cities and towns, criminals are attacking the unsuspecting, robbing people of their money, leaving them stripped, broken, bruised and half dead. Every newspaper and news magazine, every newscast, has its stories of crime. Our world today is full of pilferers, embezzlers, pickpockets, bank robbers, kidnappers, rapists, abortionists, racketeers, drug pushers, pimps, prostitutes, gangsters, killers.

So pervasive is crime in America, much of it related to drug trafficking, that our prisons are bulging. Omaha has been a relatively crime-free city. But not so long ago the *Omaha World Herald* carried a story on the Douglas County Correction Center:

> Sixty-two inmates of the Douglas County Correction Center are spending all their time in the jail's gymnasium, but not for exercise. That is where they live. In the last two months, the jail has become so overcrowded the officials have lodged inmates in almost every available corner.
>
> Said Joe Vitek, county corrections director, "We've turned the library into a dormitory. We've got people in the sixth-floor jail at the courthouse, and we've been putting people in the gym. This is an emergency situation."

It is a sad commentary on the state of our

society. But it is also a fact. As we travel in our
world today, all of us are endangered by some
of our fellow travelers who are motivated sole-
ly by criminal intent. And because of them, we
encounter only too often a second kind of
traveler.

2. Critically Wounded

A man was going down from Jerusalem to
Jericho, when he fell into the hands of robbers. They stripped him of his clothes, beat
him and went away, leaving him half
dead. (10:30)

Jesus called this traveler simply "a man." We
know no more about him than that. He was a
stranger and unknown. Whether he had been
in Jerusalem to worship or on business or to
visit friends, we do not know. We might guess
that he had been there on business and was
carrying some of his profit home to Jericho.
That made him an attractive target.

He was rather foolhardy, or he would not
have been traveling alone. In that day the wise
traveled in caravans or convoys. By making the
journey alone, he brought his trouble upon
himself.

Much of the suffering in our world is self-in-
flicted, although we do not want to admit it.
For example, the American Lung Association
reported 78,000 deaths in 1987 due to chronic

bronchitis and emphysema. And 82 percent of
the victims were smokers.

But whether the critically wounded traveler
of Jesus' story was reckless or not is not the
point. He was a man in need, a "neighbor"
who needed help and love.

"Who is my neighbor?" we ask. Jesus by His
story was saying that any human being,
stranger or acquaintance, coming across our
pathway in need of help is our neighbor. Rank,
race, religion, relationship do not matter.
Anyone who has a need we can meet becomes
our neighbor. That man or woman, youth or
child who is down, wounded, bleeding, abandoned, hurting is our neighbor. Our link with
the other person is not blood or friendship or
association; it is his or her need.

The wounded traveler may be Mary, a
mother of six children, all under the age of
eight, abandoned by her husband. Mary lost
everything in a fire. Everything. Our church
reached out to Mary and helped her get back
on her feet.

Or he may be Jim

The wounded traveler may be Jim, who came
around one afternoon to help an inner city pastor mail fliers for his church's rummage sale.
For an hour the two men talked about goals
and even about Christ. That night, under the
influence of drugs, Jim drowned in a city park
pool.

The wounded traveler may be Charles, an out-of-work father of three children. To make matters worse, Charles could neither read nor write—not even his name. The Salvation Army offered him a job and kept the family together.

The names are not real, but the people and their stories are. Each was someone's hurting neighbor.

People with similar wounds live near you or work where you do. My friend Bob moved to a new small-town neighborhood. At Christmas he and his wife invited Carolyn, a retired widow across the street, and two other neighbors for dessert and conversation. It was a pleasant evening that each seemed to enjoy. Only afterwards did Bob learn that a year earlier—at Christmastime—Carolyn's husband had committed suicide. Hardly a family has escaped a wound of one kind or another. Only as you get close to these "travelers" will you know of their personal tragedies.

Other "neighbors" may not be as close. Some are huddled in burgeoning cities—not so much out of a desire for community as in a desperate effort to make money from each other. The noise, dirt, congestion and crime dehumanize and too often destroy them.

Too many evangelicals point to rebellious Old Testament Babel, that prototype of today's city, pull their righteous robes around them, cry out with William Cowper that "God made the country and man made the tower" and drive away to their more pleasant suburban surroundings. They try to forget the hurting people who, year after year, generation after generation, crowd into noisy, foul-smelling quarters and undergo daily indignities and terrors that coarsen and too frequently brutalize them.

These are critically wounded people, and Jesus implies that because they have needs they are neighbors. What kind of a neighbor are we? The question brings us naturally to the third kind of traveler in Jesus' story. We will call these . . .

3. Calloused

> A priest happened to be going down the same road, and when he saw the man, he passed by on the other side. So too, a Levite, when he came to the place and saw him, passed by on the other side. (10:31– 32)

It could have been happenstance in Jesus' story ("by a concurrence of events" is another translation), but in real life a sovereign God orders the circumstances of our lives. Random chance does not control our world. We are not footballs that bounce here and there without rhyme or reason.

Jericho was a favorite residence for priests, and this priest evidently was returning home after serving his course of duty in the temple at Jerusalem. We should certainly have expected the priest to show kindness. He was fresh from the sanctuary and from reading Moses and the prophets. But, no! Suppose the injured man should expire while he was rendering assistance. By Old Testament Law he would be ceremonially unclean for a whole week. He was looking forward to home and family. He did not wish seven days of isolation. He dared not, therefore, help this critically wounded traveler.

Shortly after, another calloused traveler came down the road. He was a Levite—also a religious person who could be expected to help a fellow being in need. Perhaps he, too, was concerned about ceremonial cleanliness. Or perhaps he feared the robbers were looking for a second victim—or that the "wounded" man was a decoy whose cohorts were waiting to pounce on anyone foolish enough to stop. Whatever his reasons, he also decided against involvement. He also passed by on the other side.

Neither priest nor Levite wanted to risk ceremonial uncleanness, personal safety, personal expense, personal inconvenience. So they drew their righteous robes a little tighter, looked straight ahead and hurried on.

Certainly the priest and probably the Levite were returning home from an incredibly elaborate worship service at the temple. But the careful explanation of the Law and the Prophets to which they had just listened had made them no more open to their dying countryman on the Jerusalem-Jericho road. The beautiful worship service had offered them no plan of action for ministering to the hurting stranger they would soon encounter.

Overtaken by cold callousness

I fear this same cold callousness is overtaking us who call ourselves orthodox and evangelical. Are we so overcome by our awesome worship services and the spell-binding sermons preached to us that we neglect the hurting and needy in our cities and the critically wounded of our suburbs and towns?

When Donna and I moved to Omaha in 1980, what is now Christ Community Church was in the center of the inner city. The church was surrounded by hurting people. But like so many other white, Anglo-Saxon Protestant churches, our church moved to the suburbs. The move solved our parking problems and our space limitations. It brought the church nearer to the majority of its members, who by then were living in the suburbs. But it also meant the church was moving far from the critically wounded of the inner city.

I favored the move then, and I still do. But I am concerned lest the church, now comfortably located in an affluent part of Omaha, no longer feel a responsibility to our needy neighbors in the inner city. To some in our denomination, this church has been a model of evangelism and missions. But we lag when it comes to social service.

Once a month, on Communion Sunday, we take up a benevolent offering. Most people drop a dollar or two into the plate—a token offering at best, calculated to soothe their consciences. But even that is designated for those of the church congregation who meet an unexpected crisis. A few members make occasional forays into the needy areas of Omaha: the jails, the Open Door Mission. A few may help find an apartment or some furnishings for a homeless family. But those are exceptions, not the rule.

Five reasons for the problem

What is the problem? Why have white American evangelicals in this century been so reluctant to make social service a prominent part of their ministry?

Craig Ellison, professor of urban studies at Alliance Theological Seminary, suggests five reasons:

First, we have misunderstood our mandate. In our zeal to fulfill the Great Commission by making disciples, we have neglected the Great Commandment to . . . "love your neighbor as yourself." Christ never divorced the two. The Great Commission and the Great Commandment were meant to be interwoven . . .

Second, we too often have a segmented view of human beings as body and soul with a tendency to interpret the gospel in one-dimensional terms. Too often we are preaching or witnessing to "souls," leaving problems dealing with the rest of the person to other specialists—usually secular or social welfare agencies . . . There is need for each local church and every believer to reach out to the needy of our communities.

Third, we tend to interpret biblical references to the poor as meaning spiritual poverty when, in fact, Christ desires that we minister to the poor and needy in tangible ways . . .

Fourth, we white evangelicals tend to locate our churches in the suburbs where there is property but not much poverty. Then we see our fellow W.A.S.P. [white Anglo-Saxon Protestant] community [not the inner city] as our target audience . . .

Fifth, we have withdrawn from the inner cities in self-defense. In simple terms, those who have made it don't want to lose it. The cost is too high. We feel we have worked hard to get to the apex of middle-/upper- class life and don't want to give up the rewards and risk the resources. As a result, most of our middle-class churches have been uninterested in ministry to those with significant needs requiring more than an occasional guilt offering.

What, then, is the proper response to the critically wounded travelers all around us? It is found in the very practical actions of the next man along the Jerusalem-Jericho road.

4. The Compassionate

But a Samaritan, as he traveled, came where the man was; and when he saw him, he took pity on him. (10:33)

How amazing! The Samaritan could well have said, "This poor fellow is one of those Jews who will have no dealings with us Samaritans. He has often called us 'dogs.' Why should I care for him?" But, no. The two calloused religious travelers passed by on the other side; this Samaritan "came where the man was." More than that, he had compassion and pity on the hurting man.

Frequently the Old Testament prophets say God desires of His people mercy, not sacrifice. Trace the word *compassion* in the New Testament. Over and over you will find it associated with Jesus because He was the perfect incarnation of compassion.

• When [Jesus] saw the crowds, he had

compassion on them, because they were harassed and helpless, like sheep without a shepherd. (Matthew 9:36)

• When Jesus landed and saw a large crowd, he had compassion on them and healed their sick. (14:14)

• Jesus called his disciples to him and said, "I have compassion for these people; they have already been with me three days and have nothing to eat. I do not want to send them away hungry, or they may collapse on the way." (15:32)

• Jesus had compassion on [the two blind men] and touched their eyes. Immediately they received their sight. (20:34)

• A man with leprosy came to [Jesus] and begged him on his knees, "If you are willing, you can make me clean."
Filled with compassion, Jesus reached out his hand and touched the man. "I am willing," he said. "Be clean!" Immediately the leprosy left him and he was cured. (Mark 1:40–42)

A deep desire to help

Compassion in the New Testament refers to the deep-seated affections of the heart. It denotes sympathy or sorrow for the suffering and distressed. It includes with it a deep desire to help. And that is exactly what this compassionate Samaritan did. He helped the hurting stranger.

> [The Samaritan] went to him and bandaged his wounds, pouring on oil and wine. Then he put the man on his own donkey, took him to an inn and took care of him. (10:34)

Someone has suggested that if this Samaritan had lived in 20th-century America, he would have been sued for moving a critically injured victim before the medics and the ambulance arrived. But his compassion led him to *do* something. "He took care of him." The Samaritan postponed his personal plans. For the rest of that day and, indeed, throughout the night, he took care of the wounded man. Then he did something else equally costly:

> The next day he took out two silver coins and gave them to the innkeeper. "Look after him," he said, "and when I return, I will reimburse you for any extra expense you may have." (10:35)

The compassionate Samaritan not only gave of himself, risking possible assault or worse, but he gave 15–20 hours of his time and the equivalent of two days' wages—enough to keep the man for up to two months at the inn. The Samaritan must have had a good credit rating at the inn because the keeper was prepared to trust him.

The lessons for us

What lessons can we draw from Jesus' moving story about the four kinds of travelers? Is it not that you and I need to see hurting strangers as our neighbors—and then do something compassionate, caring and costly to meet their needs? Is it not that in seeking to fulfill the Great Commission in our sphere of ministry, we do it in the context and spirit of the Great Commandment?

At the close of His story, Jesus asked,

> Which of these three do you think was a neighbor to the man who fell into the hands of robbers? (10:36)

The first travelers, criminals, openly broke the law by robbing and assaulting, possibly with intent to kill. Theirs was the sin of commission. But the third travelers, a calloused priest and Levite, were also law-breakers. In doing nothing when confronted by need, they were guilty of the sin of omission.

You and I would probably never even think of breaking the law like the robbers. But could we be guilty of breaking the law like the priest and Levite—passing to the other side and doing nothing to help the person in need? Someone has suggested that the opposite of love is not always hate. Oftentimes it is indifference. It is seeing a need or a hurt and doing nothing.

At the end of the age Jesus promises to come in all His glory. He will say at that time, "I was hungry and you gave me nothing to eat, I was thirsty and you gave me nothing to drink, I was a stranger and you did not invite me in, I needed clothes and you did not clothe me, I was sick and in prison and you did not look after me. . . . I tell you the truth, whatever you did not do for one of the least of these, you did not do for me" (Matthew 25:42, 45).

John also reminds us, "If anyone has material possessions and sees his brother in need but has no pity on him, how can the love of God be in him? Dear children, let us not love with words or tongue but with actions and in truth" (1 John 3:17–18).

Bryan Jeffery Leach sums up in verse our need to rescue hurting strangers:

> Let your heart be broken
> For a world in need;
> Feed the mouths that hunger,
> Soothe the wounds that bleed,
> Give the cup of water
> And the loaf of bread—
> Be the hands of Jesus,
> Serving in His stead.

Blessed to be a blessing,
Privileged to care,
Challenged by the need—
Apparent everywhere.
Where mankind is wanting,
Fill the vacant place.
Be the means through which
The Lord reveals His grace.

Add to your believing
Deeds that prove it true,
Know the Christ as Savior,
Make Him Master, too.
Follow in His footsteps,
Go where He has trod;
In this world's great trouble
Risk yourself for God.

Let your heart be tender;
And your vision clear.
See mankind as God sees,
Serve Him far and near.
Let your heart be broken;
By a brother's pain.
Share your rich resources,
Give and give again.

(Words by Bryan Jeffery Leach, 1975. Copyright 1975 by
The Evangelical Covenant Church. Used by permission.)

Study Questions

Luke 10

1. To be out alone in what part of your city is considered unsafe? How might you or your church minister in such a difficult situation?

2. With whom do you most identify in this story: criminal, critically wounded, calloused or the compassionate?

3. What are you doing to express compassion to hurting/suffering people in your community? What more might you or your church do?

4. How does such a ministry relate to evangelism?

5. What are some of the causes which tend to make Christians or churches grow calloused in spite of a growing need for compassionate outreach for Christ into our communities?

6. Who has been a "Good Samaritan" in your life or community?

CHAPTER 12

Nurturing New Believers

Acts 2

FOR FAMILY AND FRIENDS THE BIRTH of a healthy, normal baby calls for rejoicing and celebration. But the days and weeks that follow are not usually as glorious. Incessant hunger, soiled diapers and sundry other irritations make for sleepless nights and rearranged lives. And babyhood is only the beginning! Raising that baby from infancy to maturity is no easy task!

(But babies are worth all the trouble!)

Back before fathers-to-be were present in the delivery room and sonograms were as common as they are now, three expectant fathers sat tensely in the maternity waiting room of a Minneapolis hospital. Each was anxious for word from behind the closed doors. Presently a

nurse appeared and asked to speak to the first
father.

"Is it a boy or a girl?" the man asked eagerly.

"Both!" replied the nurse. "You are the father
of twins!"

"What a coincidence!" the father exclaimed.
"I play baseball for the Minnesota *Twins!*"

The other two men had barely finished con-
gratulating the still-amazed father when
another nurse appeared with news for the
second man. His wife had just given birth to
triplets.

"This is incredible!" the shocked man replied.
"I'm employed by the *3-M* Company!"

At that point the third father bolted for the
exit.

"Hey, where are you going?" his two com-
panions called after him.

"I've gotta get out of here," the man panted,
still running. "I work for *7-Up!*"

Awesome responsibility

Imagine the awesome responsibility of
having multiple babies in your home! (Maybe
it has happened to you or to someone close to
you.) Imagine what pressures the apostles
must have felt when 3,000 spiritual babes suddenly appeared on the day of Pentecost!

Nurturing new believers is usually called
"follow-up." Without doubt, it is the most difficult and most critical aspect of evangelism.
For years I have searched for the perfect, fool-

proof, follow-up method, but in vain. No matter how careful, how loving, how diligent the follow-up efforts may be, there inevitably will be some attrition among those professing faith in Jesus Christ.

But if any group came close to the right approach, certainly it was that church of 120 believers present in the upper room when the Holy Spirit came on the day of Pentecost.

We marvel at the response to the sermon Peter preached that day. It truly was God's doing and not the result of human effort.

> Those who accepted [Peter's] message were baptized, and about three thousand were added to their number that day. (Acts 2:41)

But someone has suggested that the real miracle is found in the next verse:

> They devoted themselves to the apostles' teaching and to the fellowship, to the breaking of bread and to prayer. (2:42)

A literal translation of the Greek reads, ". . . and they were *continuing* steadfastly in the teaching of the apostles." To see 3,000 people added to the church in a day was marvelous. But to see them *"continuing* steadfastly in the teaching of the apostles" is much more amazing! Far too many of today's converts who enter the front doors of our churches within a few months are departing out the back doors.

What was the early church's secret of follow-up? What did the apostles and other leaders do to so effectively conserve the fruit of their witness? The answers to those important questions are in Acts 2. Effective follow-up can be summarized in six phrases.

1. Quality Evangelism

The best follow-up, as someone aptly said, is good evangelism. If you want to see a high percentage of the people you lead to Christ stand firm in their faith and grow to maturity, be sure that your evangelism is thorough and biblical.

Peter was a model of biblical evangelism. Notice how he preached salvation only through the death and resurrection of Jesus Christ the Lord:

> This man was handed over to you by God's set purpose and foreknowledge; and you, with the help of wicked men, put him to death by nailing him to the cross. But God raised him from the dead, freeing him from the agony of death, because it was impossible for death to keep its hold on him. (2:23–24)

Notice also that Peter called for a biblical response: repentance that would lead to forgiveness of sins and faith that would be confessed publicly by baptism.

> Peter replied, "Repent and be baptized, every one of you, in the name of Jesus Christ for the forgiveness of your sins. And you will receive the gift of the Holy Spirit. The promise is for you and your children and for all who are far off—for all whom the Lord our God will call."
> With many other words he warned them; and he pleaded with them, "Save yourselves from this corrupt generation." (2:38–40)

Too much evangelism today is geared to making it as easy as possible for people to come to Christ. But, as the saying puts it, "Easy come, easy go." *Such easy-believism evangelism too often produces still-born babies.*

Most of us are guilty

Most of us who have been active in evangelism must confess that at some time in our experience we have been guilty—consciously or unconsciously—of making things too easy for the prospective Christian. Perhaps if the person expressed an interest in the gospel we have rushed him or her through a simple prayer without clearly explaining the commitment he or she should be making. Or maybe we have soft-pedaled the seriousness and consequences of sin. We may have by-passed the repentance step, assuming the seeker understood the importance of turning from the things that displease God.

In June, 1990, I spent a week in what was then East Germany—in Karl Marx Stadt—evangelizing North Vietnamese who were working to pay off their nation's war debts. At the end of each service, our team extended an invitation. Those who wanted to inquire further were asked to remain on the main floor of the sanctuary; those ready to trust Christ for salvation were urged to meet us in a room on the second floor.

Each night we dealt carefully for at least an hour with extremely earnest and honest seekers. We gave them each a Vietnamese New Testament, reviewing with them the gospel and explaining exactly how to receive Christ. We led them individually in a prayer and then shared the five steps for growing in Christ. They each looked up the Scriptures and recorded them in the back of their New Testaments. On the front flyleaf they penned their "birth certificate," which I signed.

While leading three of the Vietnamese in prayer to receive Christ, something unusual happened. One of the three had been sobbing in repentance for her sins. Assuming the other two had an equal sense of sorrow, I had spent no time talking about sin. But as I led the three in prayer, I noticed that one of the three was not praying. I supposed she had not understood that I expected her to voice the prayer, so I asked her to repeat the words after me. She did not.

"You probably wonder why I didn't pray," she explained, "but in your prayer you said, 'Forgive me for my sins.' I am not a sinner, so I could not pray that."

Right then, before doing anything else, I discussed sin, turning to the Ten Commandments in Exodus 20 and reading them one-by-one with brief explanations. The woman admitted that she had broken them all and was indeed a sinner in need of forgiveness. Then she prayed a genuine prayer of repentance and faith.

That leads me to still a third observation. *In the spiritual realm, good soil involves the understanding.* Notice that in the description of Peter's evangelism we are told:

> With many other words [Peter] warned them; and he pleaded with them. (2:40)

Peter seems to have been careful to lead his hearers to a thorough understanding of the gospel and the commitment they were about to make.

In His explanation of the parable of the four kinds of soils, Jesus says the good soil represents the person "who hears the word and *understands* it" (Matthew 13:23). That person becomes a fruit-bearing Christian.

Whenever we evangelize, we must be sure the other person understands the gospel we are presenting and the commitment we are inviting him or her to make. If we will be thorough at these points, we will discover a much higher number of healthy births, and our follow-up task will be much easier.

2. Persistent Assimilation

If those we win to Christ are to continue to live and grow in Christ, their assimilation into the church is a must.

Assimilation begins with *baptism*.

> Those who accepted [Peter's] message were baptized. (2:41)

In His Great Commission Jesus Christ specifically commanded His followers to baptize those who became disciples: "Go and make disciples of all nations, baptizing them in the name of the Father and of the Son and of the Holy Spirit, and teaching them to obey everything I have commanded you" (Matthew 28:19–20). In fact, the wording of the commission implies that the making of disciples is accomplished by baptizing and by teaching. When we "make disciples of all nations," a part of the process is "baptizing them in the name of the Father and of the Son and of the Holy Spirit."

In New Testament times, an unbaptized believer was unthinkable. When the Ethiopian official came to faith in Christ, his first act was to be baptized (Acts 8:36–38). When Cornelius and his household trusted Christ as Savior and Lord, Peter said, "Can anyone keep these people from being baptized with water?" (Acts 10:47). When the Philippian jailer and others in his household turned to Christ, that very night "he and all his family were baptized" (Acts 16:33).

Baptism is an important opportunity for new believers to confess their faith publicly. Baptism is a step of obedience to God and the Scriptures; it solidifies the new convert's commitment to Christ and to His church.

Bring them into the church

Baptism's significance leads naturally to the next vital step in assimilating new converts. We must bring them *into the church*.

> Those who accepted [Peter's] message were baptized, and about three thousand were added to their number that day. (2:41)

Those 3,000 people who believed and were baptized were added to and assimilated into the church. Having been joined by faith to Christ, they also became joined to Christ's body, the church. It was inconceivable in the first century that true believers should not be identified with the church. Faith in Christ was synonymous with participation in His church. Coming to Christ, the Living Stone, they became living stones being built into a spiritual house—the church (1 Peter 2:4–5). Stones unjoined to one another are likely to resemble a rock quarry or a gravel pit more than a spiritual house!

I cannot overemphasize the importance of "folding" new believers into a Bible-believing, Spirit-filled, evangelistic church. Not always can you—or ought you—assimilate those you lead to Christ into your own church. But do be careful to see that they identify with, worship regularly at and become active in a spiritually solid church.

A caution. Sometimes, especially if the person has attended no church and seems hesitant to try, it is best to approach this step gradually.

In the Philippines, a nominally Roman Catholic nation, Makati Bible Church in Manila was successful in leading a number of Filipinos to Christ. But these who had found Christ resisted attending a Protestant church. So the Makati church tried something different. At first, the members helped these new believers through one-to-one Bible study. After a while, they invited them to a group Bible study—still in a private home. Gradually the teaching led to the subject of baptism. At that point, the members invited these new believers to be baptized at the church. From then on it became natural for the newly baptized believers to return to the same church regularly for worship, fellowship and ministry. They felt comfortable in the church where they had been baptized.

3. Biblical Teaching

The apostles evangelized thoroughly, baptized the new believers and assimilated them into the local church fellowship. Next they offered these new Christians solid biblical teaching:

> [The 3,000 new converts] devoted themselves to the apostles' teaching. (2:42)

It is vitally important to begin immediately to provide new believers with sound teaching appropriate to their state of growth. At first they will crave "pure spiritual milk" (1 Peter 2:2). Finally, as they mature, they will want solid food—the teaching about righteousness—spoken of in Hebrews 5:14.

At Christ Community Church we have developed a multifaceted approach to teaching new believers God's Word. In our immediate follow-up—that is, in the few minutes of conversation following their commitment to Christ—we give these new believers a Gospel of John and challenge them to read at least a chapter a day and to memorize John 3:16. We also give them a very brief Bible study in John covering six basic questions. We suggest that as they read through John, they put a mark beside any verse they do not understand. Then we arrange a follow-up meeting a week later to see how they are doing and to answer any questions.

On the return visit, we check their progress and endeavor to enroll them in a five-lesson, one-to-one Bible study with one of our volunteer "disciplers." If they are open to this, they fill out a registration card that is given to our discipleship deacons who, in turn, match the new believer with a discipler of appropriate age, sex and station in life.

When they have completed the five-week study, the several disciplers invite their new believer friends to continue to study with them, this time a slightly more difficult course prepared by the Navigators.

Concurrent with the one-to-one Bible study, we invite new believers to attend a Sunday school class called New Beginnings, especially designed for them. The subjects covered are assurance and cleansing, the Bible, prayer, worship, fellowship, sharing their faith, baptism, the Holy Spirit, church membership and stewardship. All 10 subjects are offered every Sunday; if a person should be gone one week, he or she can immediately pick up the missing subject.

290 Evangelism by the Book

During the New Beginnings cycle, new believers are encouraged to publicly confess their faith through baptism, to enlist in our next 16-week semester of personal evangelism training (Evangelism Explosion), to become members of the church and to volunteer for some type of ministry in the church. When they come to the end of the New Beginnings class, we suggest to them another appropriate Sunday school class where they can continue to grow through the study of God's Word.

In an earlier chapter of this book I told you of Russ Esch, a truck driver who came to Christ through a contact with one of our church members. The day Russ invited Christ into his life, I referred him to one of our discipling deacons and launched him in the Bible study and discipleship process described above. When he walked into my office a year later, Russ was not the same person. His life had undergone a radical transformation. He could say in Paul's words, "The old has gone, the new has come!" (2 Corinthians 5:17).

4. Loving Care

A warm, loving climate is as important to a new babe in Christ as it is to any newborn baby. Babies who are isolated from the loving association of other people do not develop normally. If new believers are to develop normally, they too need plenty of love, fellowship and personal care.

Relationships are much more important to new believers than are follow-up booklets, cassettes and other materials often squandered on new converts. The early church did not have our modern-day abundance of "tools," but they understood the importance of loving relationships.

> They devoted themselves . . . to the fellowship [and] to the breaking of bread. . . . All the believers were together and had everything in common. Selling their possessions and goods, they gave to anyone as he had need. . . .They broke bread in their homes and ate together with glad and sincere hearts. (2:42, 44–46)

I cannot overemphasize the importance of loving relationships in the nurture of new Christians. Without such care, new believers become stunted or imbalanced in their Christian life and walk.

There is a rather humorous story about a young army enlistee who, before leaving for basic training, asked his best girl to marry him. He promised to write her every day and to return as soon as possible for the wedding. Every day the young man wrote; every day the postman hand-delivered the letter to the man's fiancee. At last basic training was over and the soldier received a brief furlough. But when he arrived home, he discovered his girl had married the postman! The soldier's contact with the girl had only been by mail. The postman's had been personal.

Paul and Joyce's marriage was at a crossroads. Divorce seemed to be the only answer. The church they were attending was impersonal and offered no help. Then Joyce remembered an eight-year-old invitation her sister had extended to her to visit Omaha Gospel Tabernacle. Upon inquiry, she learned the church had moved and changed its name to Christ Community Church. Desperate for help, Joyce persuaded Paul to go with her.

"Scared to death"

"As I approached the church door," Paul remembers, "I was scared to death!" But as he mingled with the people, a fellow named Mel engaged him in conversation and made him feel welcome. It turned out to be a positive experience for both Paul and Joyce.

That next week, Donna and I visited the couple. Sitting with them in their back yard, we spent some time getting acquainted. They both mentioned how warm and friendly the church was.

"May I share with you what it is that makes our church so loving and caring?" I asked. They agreed.

As I concluded my gospel presentation, Joyce

prayed to receive Christ as her Savior. Paul, however, held back.

"Pastor, I'm just not ready," he admitted.

"If you're not ready, Paul, neither am I," I answered. "I learned a long time ago not to pick fruit until it is ripe. We'll stop right here. But when you are ready, I'll be as close as your telephone. Just give me a call and I'll come so quickly you'll think I flew here by jet!" Donna and I changed the subject and, a little later, left for home.

Paul and Joyce continued to attend our church. And a few weeks later Paul called me.

"I'm ready!" he said. Sure enough, Paul *and* his two lovely daughters were soon on their knees praying to receive Christ into their lives.

Paul and Joyce went through our New Beginnings class, enrolled in a Navigators course of Scripture memorization and then joined a home Bible study with one of our pastors. Before long they both signed up for our evangelism training and evidenced amazingly rapid spiritual growth, leading friends and associates to Christ. Fitting into responsible places of ministry and leadership within the church, they now have clearly reproduced in their lives the love and care that was so much a part of their coming to Christ and maturing in Him.

5. Effective Prayer

Prayer is as essential to new believers as are

fresh air and oxygen to new babies. By prayer spiritual life is both initiated and sustained.

My father, a missionary to Vietnam for 41 years, told me that in working with new believers, one of the first things he taught them was how to pray. He said that something dynamic seemed to happen in their lives when they began to commune with their Lord. As they voiced their simplest needs to God and saw God answer their prayers, their trust in and awareness of God increased rapidly.

When teaching new believers how to pray, it is important to let them know that they can begin praying immediately. Babies, before they can say a word, are able to communicate their feelings and needs to parents. And new believers can communicate at once with their heavenly Father. Suggest to them a few items for prayer. Pray with them in simple sentence prayers until prayer to God becomes as natural as talking to a friend. Show them how to praise God for who He is and to thank Him for what He does. As new believers see God answer prayer, their trust in Him will mature.

Several years ago John's parents, who were experiencing severe marital problems, asked him to find his own apartment and move out. John, a college student, found a mobile home and set up housekeeping.

Not long after that, one of John's neighbors with whom he drank at the local bar came to Christ and tried to get John to attend Christ

Community Church with him. But John had been raised as a Roman Catholic. He wanted no part of a Protestant church.

When a singing group, the Jeremiah People, were scheduled for a church appearance, John's neighbor tried again. John decided they could do no harm to his religious convictions, so he agreed to go with his friend. After the concert, John's neighbor invited him to meet Senior Pastor Bob Thune. The three exchanged some brief pleasantries. Suddenly John volunteered, "Boy, pastor, I need help to answer some very important questions!"

Pastor Bob arranged to visit John the next evening, bringing with him team members Joy and Marian. That evening John found answers to his questions. More importantly, he found Jesus Christ as his personal Savior. As the three visitors prepared to leave, John had another question.

"Pastor," he asked, "what do you do now when you return to the church?"

"We pray for those we have visited tonight," Pastor Bob said.

"Could you pray for my mom?" John wondered, explaining that his mother had filled out papers asking for a divorce. The three assured John that they would pray for his mother and father.

The next day, to John's great surprise, he found out his mother had torn up the papers, deciding to "make a go" of the marriage. This answer to prayer amazed John and strengthened his faith in God.

John's neighbor friend invited him to join a Bible study with seven other college students. They were in the midst of a Navigators course, "On Higher Ground," focusing on prayer. The study led him to buy a small notebook and begin logging prayer requests and answers to prayer. John included among his requests the salvation of his grandmother, who was dying of old age. To his great delight she confessed Christ as her Savior before she passed away.

Some months later John went on a trip to Yellowstone Park with two of his Bible-study friends. On that trip they made such things as the weather, accommodations and guidance matters of prayer. God miraculously answered, and John's appreciation for prayer and his faith in God continued to increase.

Subsequently, John completed training in personal evangelism. He has since gone to Bible college, married a fine Christian girl and with her is preparing for missionary service abroad. If you asked John what factor more than any other caused him as a new Christian to grow, he would be quick to point to prayer.

6. A Praiseful Congregation

That brings us naturally to the last aspect of follow-up modeled for us in Acts 2. I refer to *praise.*

They broke bread in their homes and ate
together with glad and sincere hearts,
praising God and enjoying the favor of all
the people. And the Lord added to their
number daily those who were being saved.
(2:46–47)

As I said earlier, environment is crucial to the
life, health and growth of new converts. And a
congregation's positive expressions of thanks,
praise and joy in God are another essential element of such a climate. It was so in the first-
century church.

The early church was a church full of praise.
And because it was so joyful, positive and
thankful, it continued to be a growing church.
New believers were added to it daily! People
are naturally and spiritually drawn to a church
where there is action. They thrive in that kind
of a stimulating, encouraging atmosphere.

Art served on the Omaha city council for 12
years and was director of parks and recreation
for another four years. For 40 years he
belonged to the same mainline church, singing
in the choir, teaching Sunday school, sitting on
the board and even serving on a pulpit supply
committee that sought to find pastors for some
of his denomination's smaller churches in the
city. But one day Art came to the striking impression that he was a Christian in name only.
Something was missing! So he decided to go on
a church-shopping circuit.

One October morning he visited our church. He was amazed when people greeted him in the parking lot and then at the front door. As he looked around the foyer, he was surprised to see that most people were carrying Bibles. Then a couple whom he had known from the Omaha Club spotted him and invited him to sit with them.

As a long-time choir member, Art paid special attention to the choir. He also listened intently to the organ; his wife, Marilie, was in his own church that very morning playing the organ. Art was unusually touched by the dynamic and enlivened praise.

Without a Bible

But Art's joy and exhilaration was suddenly interrupted when the pastor began his sermon by referring the congregation to their Bibles. Art was without one! He was relieved when his friend, Dillon, passed him his—opened to the sermon text. Intently Art listened to the minister's every word. He sensed a charge of excitement in the air.

"As that first breathtaking service came to an end," Art remembers today, "my shopping tour had come to an end! I knew that I had found a new church home."

A few weeks after that initial visit, an evangelism team from the church called on Art. Art knew just enough gospel language to convince the team that he was a Christian. The trouble was he could not convince himself! After the team had gone, he went into the bedroom and asked the Lord to forgive him his sins and to change his life.

"I was 60 years old when I came to Christ that night," Art testifies, quipping cheerily, "You see, it's never too late!"

Art became a regular attender at our church. At first, Marilie, because of her organist contract, came with him only on Sunday evenings. It did not take Marilie long to be enthralled with the music and the worship. When her commitment concluded, she too made the change.

Art and Marilie's son, Mark, made a living as a drummer in a music group that covered all the Omaha night clubs. But before long his life, too, was changed. He gave up his work and started playing drums in the church orchestra. He brought his wife and five children to church. As he looks back today, Mark attributes much of his growth as a new Christian to the influence of a congregation caught up in ardent praise and worship.

Meanwhile, Art committed himself to personal Bible study, enrolled in the New Beginnings class, completed the evangelism course and eventually was elected to serve on the elder board in charge of communications. His creative church ads are being used by many churches across North America because he has an innate ability to make the church and the gospel relevant to contemporary readers.

One day I asked Art what impact our congregation's praise and worship had on his life.

"Absolutely essential"

"They were absolutely essential to my Christian growth," Art responded. "They prepared my heart for the message because they made me conscious that God was there! I know of no other things that have so uplifted me, drawn me closer to the Lord and made me aware of God's presence."

But I hasten to add one more word about a congregation's praise and its influence upon the growth of both new and older Christians. It is absolutely crucial that the words of the hymns and choruses be understandable and relevant. It is very important to the spirit of the service that the melodies be singable and uplifting.

Recently I visited the church where my grandfather, 70 years earlier, had pastored. As I sat on the platform waiting to speak, I looked out over the congregation. Hardly anyone was singing. The few who were making an effort at it appeared to be—how can I say it kindly?—almost in pain as they labored to follow the difficult tune and understand the archaic English. Each of the selections was two or three centuries old.

For those who are mature in the faith and

who have a deep appreciation for the historic hymns of the faith—and I put myself in that category—such a worship service may be tolerable. But what about the non-church-going visitor or the new babe in Christ? Could they find anything inspiring to draw them to Christ and His church? Could they receive anything to build them up in the faith and attract them back to worship again with God's people? Is it any surprise that the little historic church once pastored by my grandfather is struggling to survive?

Contrast that with another church. As I write this chapter, I am flying home from a very exciting visit to a small but dynamic and growing Vietnamese church. Seldom have I heard a little congregation worship and praise with such spiritual gusto! Two years ago I visited that church when they were a congregation of about 30 people. Today the number has more than doubled. And along with the numerical growth there is very evident spiritual growth.

Acts 2 presents us with a beautiful cycle that every church today could well try to copy. Because of solid, biblical evangelism done in the power of the Holy Spirit, 3,000 people came to Christ in a single day! They were assimilated into the church through baptism, built up by biblical teaching, loved and cared for in the fellowship of believers, trained to pray and drawn into thankful, praiseful worship.

And as they were so nurtured, we are told

that they, in turn, reproduced by daily adding other new believers to their number!

May God do the same in our churches today!

Study Questions

Acts 2

1. When you lead someone to Christ, or if you were to lead someone to Christ, what do you see your responsibilities to that person to be thereafter?

2. What does your church do to follow-up new believers and what might be done to offer increased quality nurture for new babes in Christ?

3. What do you think are the chief causes for new believers disappearing from our churches or going out our "back doors"?

4. How can the quality, not quantity, of your (or your church's) evangelism be upgraded?

5. Have you personally confessed Christ in baptism since you believed? If not, why not?

6. What do you do and what does your church do to express loving care to new believers?

7. What adjectives do church visitors use to describe your worship service? Your friendly hospitality?

8. What percentage of growth has your church seen during the past 10 years and what is being done to increase and conserve the number of people turning to Christ?

CHAPTER 13

Preparing Future Evangelists

Ephesians 4

I N THIS FINAL CHAPTER I TURN to a section of Scripture that has received considerable attention in the past two decades. I have listened as preachers have preached from it. I have read what authors have had to say about it. I do not recall that any of these preachers or writers have focused on the vital role of the *evangelist* in preparing God's people for the work of the ministry.

Before I attempt to do so, I want you to have the entire section in mind:

> To each one of us grace has been given as Christ apportioned it. This is why it says:

"When he ascended on high,
he led captives in his train
and gave gifts to men."

(What does "he ascended" mean except that he also descended to the lower, earthly regions? He who descended is the very one who ascended higher than all the heavens, in order to fill the whole universe.) It was he who gave some to be apostles, some to be prophets, some to be evangelists, and some to be pastors and teachers, to prepare God's people for works of service, so that the body of Christ may be built up until we all reach unity in the faith and in the knowledge of the Son of God and become mature, attaining to the whole measure of the fullness of Christ. (Ephesians 4:7–13)

If we are going to properly prepare future evangelists for the church, there are three emphases in this section of Scripture that we must understand: *gifts*, *goals* and *growth*.

1. Gifts

In recent years there has been a refreshing, encouraging reemphasis upon the gifts of the Spirit in and for the church. It parallels the equally exciting reemphasis upon the mobilization of the laity for ministry. The gifts give that mobilization an essential, supernatural, enabling element.

Three other sections of Scripture contribute to our understanding of these spiritual gifts: Romans 12:3–8, First Corinthians 12–14 and First Peter 4:7–11. For our purposes we will confine ourselves principally to the Ephesians passage quoted above. In it Paul refers to two ways in which Christ gives. He gives gifts to men. He also gives the gift of men to the church.

a. Christ gives gifts to men

What exactly are the spiritual gifts that Jesus Christ, the Head of the church, gives to that church, which is His Body? A spiritual gift is a divine enabling or ability for service given to us through the Holy Spirit. It differs from a talent in that a talent is a natural ability that we have from birth, whereas a spiritual gift is a supernatural ability given to us at the time of or subsequent to our rebirth by the Holy Spirit.

It also seems apparent that Christ, through the Spirit, gives gifts for particular types of service. Timothy, for example, was given a spiritual gift at the time Paul laid his hands on him for ministry. Paul exhorted Timothy to "fan into flame the gift of God, which is in you through the laying on of my hands" (2 Timothy 1:6). He goes on: "God did not give us a spirit of timidity, but of power, of love and of self-discipline" (1:7).

While I was still a theological student in college, Dr. Louis L. King, pastor, missionary, missions administrator and later president of The Christian and Missionary Alliance, shared with me his personal testimony regarding Christ's granting to him the gift of an evangelist. For two years Dr. King had been serving as a young pastor, preaching the Word faithfully. But he was concerned because so few in his audiences were turning to Christ. For a long while he had made this a matter of earnest prayer, asking God to give him the gift of an evangelist.

Dr. King's ordination was approaching. He recalled that Timothy had been granted a gift when Paul laid hands on him. Dr. King fasted and prayed, asking God to give to him for his ministry the gift of an evangelist. As those of the ordaining council laid their hands upon him, setting him apart for the gospel ministry, Dr. King claimed by faith God's gift.

He returned to his pastorate. Just as before, he continued to preach the Word faithfully. But something amazing happened. From the first Sunday evening, people began coming to Christ as he preached. Eventually every week there were people converted to Christ.

Then Dr. King was sent as a missionary to India. He began preaching evangelistic messages throughout Gujarat State. Wherever he went and whenever he preached, people came to Christ in large numbers.

The gift never departed

After several years in India, Dr. King was asked to return to America to direct Alliance missions in all of Asia. Later he became vice-president for all overseas ministries of the Alliance, and finally church president. Many years after our first meeting, I asked Dr. King about the gift of evangelist. I was especially interested in knowing if he found the gift still evident now that he was an administrator. He assured me that God was still giving fruit. Whenever he had opportunity to preach evangelistically, God blessed the message with people coming to Christ.

That testimony had a tremendous impact on my life and ministry. As I studied the Scriptures, I saw clearly that all the spiritual gifts "are the work of one and the same Spirit, and he gives them to each one, just as he determines" (1 Corinthians 12:11). In other words, God is sovereign, and He gives His gifts to whomever He chooses. But He also suggests through Paul that we can "eagerly desire the greater gifts" (1 Corinthians 12:31).

As I prepared to leave for Vietnam, where I would serve as a missionary church planter, I began to eagerly desire the gift of evangelist. And as church leaders laid their hands on me for missionary service, I asked God to grant me that gift.

Later, after two years of language study, I

began to go into the villages with Vietnamese pastors and other Christians. At first, because my language ability was still limited, I preached very simple evangelistic messages— to the children. Before very long, however, adults began to crowd in among the children to hear the gospel. So the pastors asked if I would be willing to speak to adults.

One day—I can never forget it—after one of my rather faltering evangelistic messages, Pastor Dinh Thong remarked, "Missionary, I believe God has gifted you as an evangelist!" I was encouraged that one of my mentors should recognize the gift. In four years of evangelism, my associates and I were able to plant eight new churches in the province where we worked.

As the years went on, I was invited to preach in evangelistic crusades all over Vietnam. I was recognized and received by the church as a field-wide evangelist.

b. Christ gives the gift of men to the church

My experience in Vietnam brings us to another aspect of Christ's gifts to His church. Not only does He give spiritual gifts to men, but *He gives the gift of men to the church*. It was Christ who "gave some to be apostles, some to be prophets, some to be evangelists, and some to be pastors and teachers" (Ephesians 4:11).

People want to know where we get the idea of clergy from the Bible. The words *clergy* and *clergyman* do not occur in the Scriptures. But in this Ephesians letter a special group of gifted persons are designated whom God has set apart for specialized ministries within the church.

Some Bible teachers insist that the offices of apostle and prophet were established for the benefit of the church at its beginning. It was they who, under the inspiration of the Holy Spirit, penned the New Testament for our continued instruction. It was they who fanned out across the first-century world to establish the church in North Africa, in Europe and in Asia as far east as India. But now that those tasks have been accomplished, there is no further need for apostles and prophets. Consequently, God is no longer giving the church apostles and prophets. So runs the argument.

In the strictest sense, that line of reasoning is accurate. But I cannot help but believe that in a broader sense today's missionaries are the current equivalent of apostles. They serve like the early apostles at the cutting edge of church expansion. Like Paul and John and Thomas, they are pioneers taking the gospel into unpenetrated frontiers. And although we do not now need prophets who *fore*tell future events (the Bible is our sufficient revelation), we do need prophets who *forth*tell God's Word to the edifying of the church.

Paul wrote to the Corinthian believers: "Follow the way of love and eagerly desire spiritual gifts, especially the gift of prophecy. . . . Everyone who prophesies speaks to men for their strengthening, encouragement and comfort. . . . He who prophesies edifies the church" (1 Corinthians 14:1–4).

Evangelists

No one seems to question that there are evangelists in the church today. It is clear that Christ continues to give to His church evangelists. We think of men of recent history such as D. L. Moody and Billy Sunday. Billy Graham is known and respected worldwide. Louis Palau and D. James Kennedy are current well-known evangelists.

At the World Congresses on Evangelism in Berlin, Amsterdam and Manila, literally thousands of evangelists from all over the world gathered to determine how they might more effectively discharge their God-given responsibilities. They strategized how best to fulfill, within this generation, Christ's Great Commission of world evangelization.

While serving in Vietnam, I had the privilege of meeting and ministering with national evangelists whom God had gifted and given to the Vietnamese church. One of them, whom I already told you about, was 72-year-old Phan Dinh Lieu. He taught me much about sharing the gospel in his language and culture during the month he spent with me in village evangelism. In that one month alone, a hundred people turned to Christ and we planted three new churches.

"Pastors and teachers"

A fourth group, together with apostles, prophets and evangelists, whom God has given to the church are pastors and teachers. I put the two together because the Bible does. The words could be translated "shepherds and teachers." Certainly no one can question that pastors and teachers are God's gift to His church. As I see our Senior Pastor Robert Thune leading our church with vision, by example, by administrative gifts, by his relevant and biblical preaching, I praise God. Throughout our land and around the world, other godly, Spirit-filled shepherd-teachers build up the Body of Christ. We thank God for them.

2. Goals

Paul says that Christ has a specific purpose in gifting His church with apostles, prophets, evangelists and pastors and teachers. It is "to prepare God's people for works of service" (Ephesians 4:12). As I suggested earlier, little or nothing is being said about the role of the evangelist in this preparation of God's people for service. Since this is a book about evangelism, I want to focus especially on the evangelist and how the triune God desires to use him "so that the body of Christ may be built up."

a. Evangelizing

The first goal God has in mind for the evangelist is inherent in the word itself. The evangelist is to evangelize. He is to proclaim the good news, to announce salvation through Jesus Christ.

For the first two decades of my ministry, it was my privilege and joy to proclaim this good news. I saw many come to faith in Christ. I have no words to describe the personal joy that was mine each time someone confessed Jesus Christ as his Savior and Lord.

How wonderful it is that God gives this privilege and joy not to angels but to redeemed men and women. When Christ first came to earth at Bethlehem, angels announced the good news to shepherds who were watching their flocks by night. But from then until now, it has been our privilege, as human beings, to evangelize. And it has been our responsibility.

God has given the church evangelists for the purpose of evangelizing. But the Scriptures state another reason, too.

b. Equipping

> It was [Christ] who gave some . . . to be evangelists, . . . to prepare [or equip] God's people for works of service. (4:11–12)

Normally we think about the pastors and teachers as the equippers of the saints for ministry. But Paul states that evangelists are also to equip members of Christ's church for ministry. For what kind of ministry? It is logical to assume that the equipping done by evangelists should be for evangelistic ministry.

Such was Jesus' strategy with His disciples. As He went about Israel evangelizing from town to town, He equipped 12 men for evangelism through on-the-job training. After three years of preparation, He gave them a command to "make disciples of all nations" (Matthew 28:19). He told them they were to be witnesses to Him in Jerusalem, Judea, Samaria and "to the ends of the earth" (Acts 1:8). Then He Himself ascended to heaven.

In his classic *Master Plan of Evangelism*, Robert Coleman elaborates in detail on Christ's strategy. I read the book many times and preached many sermons on the importance of such an equipping ministry within the church. For 20 years I took young men with me—both pastors and laymen—as I evangelized in village after village in Vietnam. On two different occasions, in the midst of other evangelistic activity, Donna and I began youth centers where we endeavored to train young men to be evangelists. But very few of them ended up serving Christ as evangelists.

Then, in 1977, I discovered Kennedy's *Evangelism Explosion*. At last I knew exactly how to equip fellow believers—including pastors and missionaries—for a ministry of evangelism.

How eternally rewarding it has been to prepare hundreds and hundreds of God's people for evangelistic service!

3. Growth

God's purpose in emphasizing evangelism goes far beyond the rescue of sinners who otherwise are destined for eternal torment in hell. His purpose, stated in positive terms, is the building of a church comprised of these redeemed sinners—a church body that will continue to minister to one another. And it is to be a growing church body. Paul seems to suggest three kinds of growth. All three are important, and the three are interdependent: organizational growth, numerical growth and spiritual growth. Just as a stool needs at least three legs if it is to be useful, so the church needs all three kinds of growth.

a. Organizational growth

The need for organizational growth can be illustrated by pouring sand on a table. When the table has as much sand as it possibly can hold, any more is going to run over the edges and spill on the floor. The only way that flat table surface can hold more sand is for it to be expanded, adding to length or width or both.

Likewise the ministers—clergy or lay—in a given church can minister effectively to only so many people. If the church wants to win and disciple more people, it must add more workers.

The Ephesians passage we have been looking at suggests a strategy for growth. It is the training or equipping of rank-and-file members for ministry. Organizationally, the apostles, prophets, evangelists and pastors and teachers equip lay people for ministry.

In our Omaha church we are careful not to call our pastors "ministers." We regard our lay people as the ministers of Christ Community Church. We who are the pastors are there to train them for their ministry.

When I moved to Omaha in 1980, I began immediately training members to be lay ministers who would work with me in evangelism. After a few years of this, I also enlisted, trained and oversaw a group of "outreach elders," now seven in number. These outreach elders oversee seven specific areas of our church's outreach ministry: visitor relations, evangelism, discipleship, social service, church planting, world missions and missionary giving.

Before long, however, these outreach elders discovered that owing to church growth they could not manage their areas of ministry alone. The "sand" on the "table" was at maximum. So we began to enlist and prepare deacons, people we regard as "assistant elders," who are helping their elder in the administration of a more specialized or limited area of his responsibility. For example, the elder for visitor relations has deacons who oversee the parking lot, the before-service greeting of visitors, the after-service visitor reception and a "welcome class" we make available for interested visitors.

As pastor for outreach, I now spend most of my time enlisting workers, equipping them and directing the outreach ministry at large. Others care for the details. And when it comes to the equipping, my first tool is Evangelism Explosion.

I am convinced that Jesus began the training of His disciples by equipping them for evangelism. He enlisted a group of men to be His future apostles or leaders, and He trained them, as He promised, to be "fishers of men" (Mark 1:17). When they proved themselves in evangelism, He added additional responsibilities. *All* of the apostles, therefore, were trained in evangelism.

We know relatively little about the seven deacons chosen by the early church to oversee food distribution. But we are told in considerable detail how both Stephen and Philip evangelized. We have no detail regarding the training of early church elders, but Peter refers to their witness (1 Peter 5:1). Before he says anything about their willingness to serve, their Christian walk or their work, he calls attention to their witness. He refers to himself as their "fellow elder" and "witness."

My second tool for preparing the leaders with whom I work is called *Master Planning*. It was developed by Bobb Biehl of Masterplanning Associates, Laguna Niguel, California. I find it valuable for training leaders to oversee their own lives and ministry and, in turn, to equip and lead the deacons with whom they serve. All of this contributes to the organizational growth of our church.

b. Numerical growth

It also contributes to our church's numerical growth. Unfortunately, there are Christians today who want nothing to do with numbers. They feel that to focus on numerical growth in the church is carnal. It is "bringing Madison Avenue into the church." These critics fail to see that the Bible is full of numbers. The Acts described in careful detail the numerical growth of the early church. Luke, the book's human author under God, was a doctor accustomed to keeping accurate statistics. Doctors cannot function without numbers and statistics.

Certainly we are not to seek numerical growth for human glory. Pride should have no place in the advance of Christ's church. But every number added to the total represents another precious person for whom Christ died. Those who disparage numbers may simply be trying to hide their own failure to reach out to lost people.

I am excited to be part of a church that believes in setting numerical goals. For eight consecutive years Christ Community Church has grown at a rate of 10 percent per year. In 1990, we increased our growth rate goal to 20 percent! We have also set a goal of 5,000 members by the year 2000. And having set this faith goal, our membership is praying, planning and working with that end in view—for God's glory and the extension of His kingdom.

It is my conviction that organizational growth can greatly enhance numerical growth in very biblical and spiritual ways. In an earlier chapter I referred to Robert Orr of the Institute for American Church Growth, Monrovia, California, who told me if he were the pastor of a church, his *first* staff addition would be a pastor for outreach. I believe more churches should consider adding such a team member. I like the title "Outreach Pastor" or "Associate Pastor for Outreach" rather than "Minister of Evangelism" because his focus should be broader than just evangelism. It should include visitor relations, evangelism, discipleship, church planting, social service and world missions. (And the members, not the clergy, should be the "ministers"!)

Where will they come from?

Regrettably, there are not many pastors trained or being trained to oversee church outreach. There are many who can lead an Evangelism Explosion ministry. That is an important facet of outreach, but it is only one facet. Our seminaries are not producing men trained to lead in outreach. They cannot. No classroom can adequately equip such a person. Where, then, does a church look for such a pastor?

New Testament evangelists were to equip other leaders in the church body through on-the-job training. So outreach pastors must reproduce themselves by the on-the-job training of other outreach pastors.

With this in mind, we have developed an internship program within the outreach ministry of Christ Community Church. Some of these interns are from our own ranks; others come in from the outside to receive on-site training. As we train them, we are endeavoring to instill in them the pattern of New Testament church growth so that they, in turn, will also train others in outreach. These internees are now beginning to go out from our church to other congregations anxious to grow in the New Testament way.

In an earlier chapter I alluded to Fred, who with his wife, Peggy, came to Christ through our E.E. ministry and later became an E.E. teacher/trainer and a church elder. Today he serves as an outreach pastor in an East Coast church.

Fred's growth and usefulness challenged me to train others. Gerry was one whom God clearly sent our way. Following graduation from Grace College of the Bible in Omaha, Gerry and his wife Becky continued to attend

Christ Community Church, both enrolling in our evangelism training. One day after leading a fellow security guard where he worked to Christ, Gerry called me for an appointment.

Gerry was hardly seated in my office when he began.

"Pastor Tom, for some time I haven't been able to decide what to do with my life. But since God has used me to bring people to Christ, I feel God leading me to do this full-time! Would you be willing to train me to be an outreach pastor like yourself?"

"Gerry," I responded, looking him straight in the eye, "if you will give a year of your life to such training and follow the ministry disciplines I will outline, I'll work with you."

It was a deal

It was a deal. Gerry attended our annual evangelism leadership training clinic. He started teaching evangelism classes and began discipling new Christians. Next, I trained him in masterplanning so he could administer our fall "evangelism spectacular." He gathered a group of couples to become his prayer support group. He became leader of one of our social service ministries.

When Gerry demonstrated real leadership qualities, I took him to Fort Lauderdale to be trained as a national clinic teacher. I gave him opportunity to coteach a clinic. Finally, he accompanied me to the Philippines to train

Filipinos in another clinic and to gain cross-cultural experience.

As I write, Gerry is candidating in a couple of fine churches that are looking for an outreach pastor. He should soon be off and running in his own ministry of outreach.

Scott is another intern, a young pastor from Washington state who feels called to specialize in outreach. He and his wife moved here to Omaha, where he has done everything Gerry did—and one thing more: Scott is helping us give birth to our church's ninth "daughter" church. He is taking two E.E. teams to a town a half hour's drive northeast, where a Bible study is already attended by 25 people. In a short time, Scott, too, will be ready to take an outreach position in another church.

What especially excites me is to learn that these interns—and five others who are training at a slower pace because of their secular work commitments—intend to do the same thing where they serve. They plan to reproduce other outreach pastors through on-the-job training.

It is my dream that hundreds and hundreds of churches will one day soon have outreach associates serving side by side with the senior pastor, leading their churches in unprecedented numerical growth.

c. Spiritual growth

At the same time we are concerned about numerical growth, we must be equally concerned about spiritual growth. The biblical objective is spiritual growth:

> . . . so that the body of Christ may be built up until we all reach unity in the faith and in the knowledge of the Son of God and become mature, attaining to the whole measure of the fullness of Christ. (4:12–13)

Christians somehow have become self-deceived. They think that daily devotions, a sermon or two each Sunday, perhaps a home Bible study and maybe a prophecy conference or two will result in spiritual maturity. They forget that all of that wonderful spiritual intake—and I disparage none of it—must be balanced by an equal amount of spiritual exercise or they will grow soft, fat and flabby.

In His high priestly prayer recorded in John 17, Jesus set forth a perfect model for Christians' priorities and balance. First, they must grow in their relationship with and knowledge of God. "This is eternal life: that they may know you, the only true God, and Jesus Christ, whom you have sent" (17:3).

Second, they must grow in their relationships with fellow believers in the church through the nurture of God's Word. "I have revealed you to those whom you gave me out of the world. They were yours; you gave them to me and they have obeyed your word. . . . Holy Father, protect them by the power of your name—the name you gave me—so that they may be one as we are one" (17:6, 11).

Third, they must go with the gospel into that part of the world—usually right at home— where Jesus sends them. "My prayer is not that you take them out of the world but that you protect them from the evil one. . . . As you sent me into the world, I have sent them into the world. . . . My prayer is not for them alone. I pray also for those who will believe in me through their message" (17:15, 18, 20).

It has been my observation and experience through the years that when believers keep these three priorities in proper balance and in that order, they will evidence true spiritual maturity. Other books deal at length with the first two priorities. Because evangelism and disciple-making are the special theme of this book, I want to amplify that third point.

Evangelism is crucial to spiritual maturity

Evangelism and disciple-making are crucial to spiritual maturity for several reasons.

In learning a "formulation" of the gospel and in sharing it with others we *grow in spiritual security*. We are sharing our personal testimony—how we discovered eternal life. We are quoting the Scriptures that speak of eternal life. We are using illustrations about eternal life. We are helping others reach assurance of eternal life. All these things strengthen our own sense of security in Christ Jesus.

We also *experience* a more real and personal *sense of Christ's presence*. Christ's Great Commission was both a command and a promise. He said, "All authority in heaven and on earth has been given to me. Therefore go and make disciples of all nations, baptizing them in the name of the Father and of the Son and of the Holy Spirit, and teaching them to obey everything I have commanded you. And surely I am with you always, to the very end of the age" (Matthew 28:18–20). To whom does Jesus promise His presence? Is it not to those who obey His command to go and make disciples? Why should we expect to experience intimacy with Christ if we are not actively involved in the work closest to His heart?

Third, we *receive increased spiritual power* when we are involved in evangelism and discipling. Christ promised to link the power of His Spirit with our witnessing: "You will receive power when the Holy Spirit comes on you; and you will be my witnesses" (Acts 1:8). It is inconceivable that believers can claim to be filled with the Spirit if they are not actively sharing their faith in obedience to Christ's command. The book of Acts is an account of a church that was obediently witnessing in the power of the Spirit. Peter testified to this truth when he declared, "We are witnesses of these things, and so is the Holy Spirit, whom God has given to those who obey him" (Acts 5:32).

Fourth, as we become involved in evangelism

and discipling we *discover joyful unity* in the body of Christ. When the early church was scattered as a result of great persecution, the members had every reason to complain. Instead, we learn that "those who had been scattered preached the word wherever they went. Philip went down to a city in Samaria and proclaimed the Christ there. . . . So there was great joy in that city" (Acts 8:4–5, 8). Filled with God's Spirit and witnessing to what Christ had done in their lives, these believers had no time to complain, to criticize or to say cutting things to or about one another. What wonderful joy and unity were evident in their lives!

Human behavior oftentimes does not differ very much from that of our animal friends. Put two or three bird dogs or a few monkeys in a cage and watch what happens. With nothing to hunt for, the dogs will start growling at and biting each other. The monkeys, used to taking care of their own fleas, suddenly start looking for and picking at the fleas on the other monkeys. Christians who are actively sharing Christ outside the walls of their churches generally do not have the time, interest or energy to be concerned about someone else's quirks or faults. Rather, they focus on the unity and mutual joy they share in the fellowship of the gospel.

Fifth, when we are involved in evangelism and discipling we *gain spiritual understanding.* We will gain understanding of our spiritual gifts, of God's truth, of our own role in spiritual ministry. Paul wrote of this to one of his brothers in Christ. He said, "I pray that you may be active in sharing your faith, so that you will have a full understanding of every good thing we have in Christ" (Philemon 6).

Often I have seen this principle at work in new believers. One young man, Mike, comes to mind. He first came to our church as a long-haired, typical "hippie." After he found Christ, he soon became involved in a witnessing, discipling fellowship. God began to speak to him about full-time Christian service. He enrolled in Bible college, married a lovely, Spirit-filled girl, went on to seminary and today is serving as a missionary in Africa. I have seen literally hundreds of examples of this kind of growth in spiritual understanding.

Evangelism is fulfilling

Finally, when we are involved in evangelism and discipling, we *enjoy personal fulfillment* seldom experienced in any other way. There are only two things in this world that are eternal: the living, enduring Word of God and never-dying people who will be resurrected to live forever in heaven or hell. When we lead a person to Christ and disciple him or her to maturity, we are doing something of eternal worth. Forever and ever, as we meet that person in heaven, we will have the satisfaction of knowing our witness made the difference in his or her destiny. That is purpose and fulfillment beyond description! How many times I have heard someone exclaim, just after he or she won a person to Christ, "I'll never be the same! There's just nothing to compare with it!"

That brings me back to the thesis and theme of this book. Let me encourage you to discover, if you have not, this fulfilling ministry of evangelism and disciple-making. Together we have looked at the pattern modeled by our Lord Jesus Christ, His apostles and the first-century church. We have reviewed Jesus' Great Commission. I have shared with you many of my own experiences in this fulfilling pursuit. I have introduced you to Evangelism Explosion, a carefully crafted plan to thoroughly prepare you to lead people to Christ. Through the example of Christ Community Church in Omaha, where I am Associate Pastor for Outreach, I have tried to draw open the curtain on some of the exciting possibilities when a whole congregation becomes involved in evangelism and the making of disciples.

I come from a good family; I thank God for my family heritage. But it was not an inborn or natural talent that qualified me for the ministry I have had. Apart from the Holy Spirit and the spiritual gifts God gave me, I could have accomplished little.

You serve the same God I do. You are under the same Great Commission; you have the same Holy Spirit. Your church has the same potential to grow and to impact this generation and world for Christ.

I challenge you to get alone with God. Open your Bible to Matthew 28:19–20 and Christ's last command. Ask God to help you dream some really big dreams: dreams of captive sinners being gloriously set free, dreams of ordinary but Spirit-filled people being equipped as successful fishers of men, dreams of barren branches being pruned and producing abundantly, dreams of eternal trophies—people—won to Jesus Christ. Then watch God do through you evangelistic and discipling exploits so amazing you will hardly believe it!

Remember the Chinese proverb: *The longest journey begins with a single step.* Take that first step. And the next. And the next.

You, too, can experience a ministry beyond your wildest dreams!

Study Questions

Ephesians 4

1. What do you understand to be the responsibility of the evangelist in verses 7–13?
2. How is this similar or different from the pastor/teacher's responsibility (11)?
3. What do you understand a gift of the Spirit to be and for what purpose?
4. What do you perceive your spiritual gift(s) to be and how are you employing it (them)?

5. If gifts are sovereignly distributed by God, is it in order for you to seek one of the better gifts for service to Christ and His Body? Explain your reasons.

6. Would an evangelist or outreach pastor provide a valuable ministry to your church? If so, what would you envision his responsibilities to be?

7. What are the three major types of church growth set forth in Scripture and evident in truly growing churches today?

8. In what ways will a Christian grow as a result of being directly involved in personal evangelism?

Do You Know
for Sure?

DO YOU KNOW FOR SURE that you are going to be with God in heaven? If God were to ask you, "Why should I let you into my heaven?" what would you say?

If you are uncertain or hesitant—even for a moment—to answer that question, you are about to read the best news you could ever hear! The few minutes it will take you to read these pages may be the most important time you will ever spend!

Did you know the Bible tells how you can know for sure that you have eternal life and will go to be with God in heaven? "I write these things to you . . . so that you may know that you have eternal life" (1 John 5:13).

Here is how you can know for sure.

1. *Heaven (eternal life) is a free gift*. The Bible says, "The gift of God is eternal life in Christ Jesus our Lord" (Romans 6:23).

And because heaven is a gift like any other genuine gift, *it is not earned or deserved*. Therefore, no amount of personal effort, good works or religious deeds can earn a place in heaven for you. "By grace you have been saved, through faith—and this not from yourselves, it is the gift of God—not by works, so that no one can boast" (Ephesians 2:8–9). ·

Why can you not earn your way to heaven? Because . . .

2. *Like everyone else, you are a sinner.* The Bible declares, "All have sinned and fall short of the glory of God" (Romans 3:23).

Sin is transgressing God's law and includes such things as lying, lust, cheating, deceit, anger, evil thoughts, immoral behavior and more. And because of transgressions like these, *you cannot save yourself.*

If you wanted to save yourself by good deeds, do you know how good you would have to be? The Bible says you would have to be *perfect.* "Be perfect, therefore, as your heavenly Father is perfect" (Matthew 5:48).

With such a high standard, you cannot save yourself, for God also says, "Whoever keeps the whole law and yet stumbles at just one point is guilty of breaking all of it" (James 2:10).

In spite of your sin, however,

3. *God is merciful. He does not want to punish you.* This is because "God is love" (1 John 4:8) and

He says, "I have loved you with an everlasting love" (Jeremiah 31:3).

But the same Bible that tells us that God loves us also tells us that *God is just, and therefore He must punish sin.* He says, "He does not leave the guilty unpunished" (Exodus 34:7) and "The soul who sins is the one who will die" (Ezekiel 18:4).

We have a problem: We have all sinned. The penalty for sin is death. We need forgiveness so that we can have a right relationship with God. *God solved this problem for us in the Person of . . .*

4. *Jesus Christ the Lord.* Exactly who would you say Jesus Christ is? The Bible tells us clearly that He is the infinite God-Man: "In the beginning was the Word [Jesus], and the Word [Jesus] was with God, and the Word [Jesus] was God. . . . The Word [Jesus] became flesh and made his dwelling among us" (John 1:1, 14).

Jesus Christ came to earth and lived a sinless life. But while He was on earth, *what did He do?* He died on the cross to pay the penalty for your sins and rose from the grave to purchase a place for you in heaven. "We all, like sheep, have gone astray,/ each of us has turned to his own way;/ and the LORD has laid on him [Jesus]/ the iniquity of us all" (Isaiah 53:6).

God hates your sins. Because of His love for you, He has placed those sins on His Son. Christ Jesus bore your sin in His body on the

cross. Therefore He is offering you eternal life—heaven—as a free gift!
This gift is received by . . .

5. *Faith.* Faith is the key that will open the door to heaven for you. Many people mistake two things for saving faith:

a. Mere *intellectual assent,* that is, believing certain historical facts. The Bible says the devil believes in God, so believing in God is not saving faith.

b. Mere *temporal faith,* that is, trusting God for temporary crises such as financial, family or physical needs. It is good for you to trust Christ for these things, but this is not saving faith.

Saving faith is trusting in Jesus Christ alone for salvation. It means resting upon Christ alone and what He has done rather than upon what you have done to get yourself into heaven. "Believe [trust] in the Lord Jesus, and you will be saved" (Acts 16:31).

Faith is like the hand of a beggar receiving the gift of a king. We do not deserve the gift of eternal life. But we can have it if we will receive it by faith.

You have just read the greatest story ever told about the greatest offer ever made by the greatest Person who ever lived—Jesus Christ the Lord. The question that God is asking you now is, *Would you like to receive the gift of eternal life?*

Because this is such an important matter, let us clarify what it involves.

a. It means, first, that you *transfer your trust* from what you have been doing to what Christ has done for you on the cross.

b. It means, next, that you *receive the resurrected, living Christ into your life as Savior.* Jesus says, "Here I am! I stand at the door [of your life] and knock. If anyone hears my voice and opens the door, I will come in" (Revelation 3:20).

c. It means further that you *receive Jesus Christ into your life as Lord.* He comes as Master and King. There is a throne room in your heart, and that throne rightly belongs to Jesus. He made you. He bought you and He wants to take His rightful place on the throne of your life.

d. It means, finally, that you *repent of your sins.* By that you turn from anything you have been doing that is not pleasing to God and you follow Him as He reveals His will to you in His Word.

6. *Prayer.* Now, if you really want eternal life, *you can pray to God right where you are.* Right now you can receive His gift of eternal life through Jesus Christ.

It is with your heart that you believe and are justified, and it is with your mouth that you confess and are saved . . . "Everyone who calls on the name of the Lord will be saved" (Romans 10:10, 13).

If you want to receive the gift of eternal life through Jesus Christ, then call on Him, asking Him for this gift right now.

Here is a suggested prayer:

Lord Jesus Christ, I know I am a sinner and do not deserve eternal life. But I believe You died and rose from the grave to purchase a place in heaven for me. Lord Jesus, come into my life; take control of my life; forgive my sins and save me. I repent of my sins and now place my trust in You for my salvation. I accept Your free gift of eternal life. Amen.

If that prayer is the desire of your heart, look at what Jesus promises to those who believe in Him: "I tell you the truth, he who believes has everlasting life" (John 6:47).

7. *Welcome to God's family!* If you have truly repented of (forsaken, turned away from) your sins, placed your trust in Jesus Christ's sacrificial death and received the gift of eternal life, you are now a child of God! Forever! Welcome to the family!

"To all who received him, to those who believed in his name, he gave the right to become children of God" (John 1:12).

8. *Today is your spiritual birthday*—a day you will want to remember always! "Born, not of natural descent, nor of human decision or a husband's will, but born of God" (John 1:13).

When you were physically born, the day of your birth was attested by a birth certificate.

And so, today, to help you recall what God has done in your life on this important day, we invite you to sign and keep the *Spiritual Birth Certificate :*

SPIRITUAL BIRTH CERTIFICATE

"Everyone who calls on the name of the Lord will be saved" (Romans 10:13).

Knowing that I have sinned and that I need the Lord Jesus Christ as my Savior, I now turn from my sins and trust Jesus for my eternal life. I ask Jesus Christ to forgive me and to deliver me from sin's power and to give me eternal life.

I now give Jesus Christ control of my life.

From this time forward, as God gives me strength, I will seek to serve Him and obey Him in all areas of my life.

Signature _____

Date _____

---

9. *What is next?* Just as a newborn baby grows physically, so you will grow spiritually by taking the following steps:

a. Read one chapter of the book of John (in the Bible) each day. "Like newborn babies, crave pure spiritual milk, so that by it you may grow up in your salvation" (1 Peter 2:2).
b. Spend time each day in prayer, conversing with God. "Do not be anxious about anything, but in everything, by prayer and petition, with thanksgiving, present your requests to God" (Philippians 4:6).
c. Worship regularly in a church that teaches you the Bible and honors Jesus Christ. "I rejoice with those who said to me,/ 'Let us go to the house of the Lord' " (Psalm 122:1).

"God is Spirit, and his worshipers must worship in spirit and in truth" (John 4:24).

"Let us not give up meeting together, as some are in the habit of doing" (Hebrews 10:25).
d. Fellowship with Christians who will help you grow in faith. "Those who accepted [Peter's] message . . . devoted themselves to the apostles' teaching and to the fellowship, to the breaking of bread and to prayer" (Acts 2:41–42).
e. Be a witness by telling others what Jesus Christ means to you.

Jesus said, "Whoever acknowledges me before men, I will also acknowledge him before my Father in heaven. But whoever disowns me before men, I will disown him before my Father in heaven" (Matthew 10:32–33).

Copyright by Evangelism Explosion III International.
Used with permission.